Pursuing Purity
and Spiritual Beauty

Pursuing Purity
and Spiritual Beauty

Virginia Lefler

Silverday Press
P. O. Box 1011
Downers Grove, IL 60515

For up-to-date information about
Silverday Press, or to obtain more
information about this book, visit
www.SilverdayPress.com

Pursuing Purity and Spiritual Beauty

(formerly *Pursuing Purity*)

Published by Silverday Press — www.SilverdayPress.com

Printed in the United States of America.

Library of Congress Control Number: 2009909424

ISBN: 978-0-9729903-5-6

Cover Design: Pam Hamilton
                  www.pamhamdesign.com

Contents

Dear Sisters in Christ,

Pursuing Purity and Spiritual Beauty is a revised and expanded version of *Pursuing Purity*. The title was changed in response to women who thought the book was only about sexual purity. Purity is a much broader topic. *Pursuing Purity and Spiritual Beauty* will help you understand the need for purifying your thoughts, words, motives and heart, and help you know how to do that. The result is an inner beauty that never fades.

We read in 1 Corinthians 2:7 that God offers us a "secret wisdom" that has been hidden from the world and that God destined for our glory before time began. Today the wisdom of purity is certainly a well-kept secret. It is my prayer that *Pursuing Purity and Spiritual Beauty* will open your eyes in a greater way to the beauty and power of purity, and that you will enjoy inner beauty more and more!

I invite you to visit my website, www.SilverdayPress.com, for a free group study guide and free audio lessons that introduce this study of *Pursuing Purity and Spiritual Beauty*. You will find them under "**Free Resources**." Also available is a study guide designed for moms and their teen daughters.

With love,

Virginia Lefler

– Chapter 1 –

The Privilege of Purity

What thoughts come to mind when you hear the word "purity"? Is it a positive word to you? If you were discussing the environment, you would most likely think of purity as an advantage or privilege because a pure environment is essential for good health. A great deal of effort has been made to educate people about our environment. This education has helped us have a greater appreciation for pure water and pure air, and to take steps to protect and clean our environment. However, purity in the context of our spiritual lives is not always associated with privilege. This is because there are obstacles that can keep us from seeing the truth about spiritual purity and the many ways it can enrich our lives.

Deception: Worldliness makes you strong.

A widely accepted myth claims that a worldly woman is strong and secure, while a woman who pursues purity is naïve and vulnerable. Movies, magazines and television all promote this message. However, if we closely examine this myth, we can see it is not true. A better way to describe a worldly woman is hardened, not strong. The Bible describes a hardening process that goes on in our hearts when we sin (Hebrews 3:7-13), and the more we sin, the harder our hearts become. The result is rivalry, jealousy, self-hatred and indifference – not strength or security.

We can look at examples all around us to see that worldliness does not make us strong. In Hollywood, for example, we have seen young stars at the age of eighteen begin to embrace more and more worldliness in order to promote their careers to adult audiences; yet their lives do not exemplify strength. Many times the result is just the opposite. Their lives are on the edge of destruction because of their choices. Some young stars get to a point where they desperately need to purify some aspect of their lives or they will soon be destroyed. They may be beautiful, talented and successful in their careers, but these things do not produce strength.

These are extreme cases, but there are less obvious examples all around us. We can look at the lives and relationships of worldly women and see their need for more strength. Their worldliness has not made them stronger women. It has actually eroded the quality of their lives.

Challenge: Purity has been too narrowly defined

Many people think of purity only as sexual purity. However, spiritual purity includes pure motives, pure speech, pure thoughts, a pure heart and more. The problem of limiting our view of purity to sexual purity is that it changes how you read and process certain scriptures. The danger of this is that a Christian can be abstaining from premarital sex or adulterous sex, but still be living a very impure life. We will see throughout this study that we are called to purify every area of our lives.

Another problem of defining purity too narrowly is a tendency for some people to give up on the idea of obeying God. They think it's too late to be pure. But that is not true. No matter what your age or what you have done in your life, it's never too late to pursue purity and to begin enjoying the benefits and promises of God.

As a Christian, purity is one of our greatest challenges, no matter how old we are or whether or not we are married. If you are young, put your whole heart into striving for purity. It won't be any easier when you are older or get married. Putting off pursuing purity is like saying you plan to wait till you are old to begin exercising. That is not a good plan! And if you put off becoming pure, it will not only be more difficult when you are older, you will also miss many blessings throughout your life.

Challenge: The changing moral standards

Another difficulty we face regarding our purity is the shifting standard of what is morally acceptable. Many things that were not acceptable forty years ago are now part of our popular culture. This is true of our entertainment, fashion, dating and marriage relationships. In 2003, it was reported that 60% of our nation believed that cohabitation before marriage was morally acceptable, 40% believed adultery was morally acceptable, and 30% believed homosexuality was morally acceptable.[1] Forty years ago, the standards for morality were higher. Our moral standards are moving but not in God's direction. Yet God's standards do not change:

> *Do you not know that the wicked will not inherit the kingdom of God? <u>Do not be deceived</u>: Neither the sexually immoral nor idolaters nor adulterers nor male prostitutes nor homosexual offenders nor thieves nor the greedy nor drunkards nor slanderers nor swindlers will inherit the kingdom of God.* [Emphasis added.]
>
> 1 Corinthians 6:9-10

This scripture warns us of two things. First, we can be deceived about what is morally acceptable. Second, there is a high cost of impurity – it can cost us heaven. Despite this, our moral standards have continued to move away from God's standards. This makes the battle for purity even more challenging, and it becomes more important than ever that we are aware of it. As moral standards decay, we need to be all the more engaged in this spiritual battle.

Since there is a moving standard, what should our goal be regarding our level of purity? Do we strive for the standards of fifty years ago or even a hundred years ago? To answer this, let me ask you another question: How pure do you want your water to be? If I offered you a choice of two glasses of water, one from a contaminated water supply and the other of pure water, which would you choose? Of course you would choose the pure water, and the purer the water the better! Our need for purity in our environment is obvious, but that is not true of our spiritual purity. So we must become as educated about our need for spiritual purity as our need for a healthy and pure environment.

The Bible has a lot to say about purity and offers us wisdom to fight this battle. It evens answers the above question regarding the level of purity we should aim for:

> *Dear friends, now we are children of God, and what we will be has not yet been made known. But we know that when he appears, we shall be like him, for we shall see him as he is. Everyone who has this hope in him <u>purifies</u> himself, just as he is <u>pure</u>.* [Emphasis added.]
>
> 1 John 3:2-3

This verse tells us that God is our standard, so our spiritual goal is absolute purity. That helps us see why we don't look back fifty or one hundred years to set our standards. Instead, we go right to the source of true purity – our goal is to become pure like God. This may seem unrealistic, but remember the benefits we enjoy in a pure environment. The greater the purity, the greater the benefits! Spiritual purity is far more important, and offers amazing blessings that we do not want to miss.

Let's consider some of the blessings we gain from purity. The number one benefit is that the pure in heart will see God (Matthew 5:8). And if that were the only blessing of purity, it would be more than enough. That will be an incredible day when we get to go before God. But this is not the only benefit. There are many more blessings we can enjoy each day. One daily benefit we enjoy is the Holy Spirit. Consider the following verses about the Holy Spirit:

> *Peter replied, "Repent and be baptized, every one of you, in the name of Jesus Christ for the forgiveness of your sins. And <u>you will receive the gift of the Holy Spirit.</u>"* [Emphasis added.]
>
> Acts 2:38

> *But <u>the fruit of the Spirit</u> is love, joy, peace, patience, kindness, goodness, faithfulness, gentleness and self-control. Against such things there is no law. Those who belong to Christ Jesus have crucified the sinful nature with its passions and desires. Since we live by the Spirit, let us <u>keep in step with the Spirit</u>.* [Emphasis added.]
>
> Galatians 5:22-25

*For God did not give us a spirit of timidity, but a <u>spirit of power,</u>
<u>of love</u> and of <u>self-discipline</u>.* [Emphasis added.]

2 Timothy 1:7

We often honor someone who has been baptized by giving them little gifts to commemorate the occasion. God goes all out to commemorate this special event – he gives them the gift of the Holy Spirit (Acts 2:38). You will receive no greater gift in your lifetime! And this gift does not sit on a shelf. No, the Holy Spirit will strengthen you (Ephesians 3:16), guide you (John 16:13) and help you overcome sin (Romans 8:13). You could not even begin to purify yourself without this gift from God. And it not only helps you overcome sin, it also fills you with the best things in life: love, joy, peace, patience, kindness, goodness, faithfulness, gentleness and self-control.

Imagine living a life void of any of these qualities. Life without one of them would have challenges. For example, consider all the ways the quality of self-control helps us have a better life. The same is true of every one of these qualities. These are blessings we can enjoy every day.

Deception: Purity means you will miss out on life

Many see spiritual purity as a price to pay, and fear they will miss out on something exciting if they choose to live a pure life. This is a powerful deception because no one wants to miss out on life. But this is just another one of Satan's schemes. Would you feel like you were missing out if you did *not* get to drink dirty water or breathe dirty air? Would your life be incomplete without this experience? Of course not! Purity in our environment is a privilege. The same is true of our spiritual purity. It is not a price to pay, but rather the path to a privileged life. Those who choose not to pursue purity are missing out on some of life's greatest blessings. Consider both God's promises and the call to purity in the following passage:

*. . . As God has said: "<u>I will live with them</u> and <u>walk among</u>
<u>them</u>, and <u>I will be their God</u>, and <u>they will be my people</u>."*

*"Therefore come out from them and be separate, says the Lord.
Touch no unclean thing, and <u>I will receive you</u>."*

"I will be a Father to you, and you will be my sons and daughters, says the Lord Almighty."

Since we have these promises, dear friends, let us purify ourselves from everything that contaminates body and spirit, perfecting holiness out of reverence for God. [Emphasis added.]

2 Corinthians 6:16 - 7:1

Promises:
I will live with you.
I will walk with you.
I will receive you.
You will be my daughters.

God is offering himself to you in a loving, nurturing relationship – a Father/child relationship. He also promises to live with you, walk with you and receive you. These are great promises. I especially like the one that says he will receive me. Knowing the Lord Almighty will receive me is very comforting. If I went to Washington to see the President, I don't think there is much of a chance that he would receive me. I doubt that the Governor or Mayor would answer my phone calls either. But the Lord Almighty has made me a promise that he will receive me. He receives my prayers every day, and someday he will receive my soul. And until that day comes, he promises to live with me, walk with me and be my Father.

Notice that the Lord *Almighty* makes these promises to us. He wants us to know that these are not empty words. He can back up his promises. He is powerful:

Lift your eyes and look to the heavens: Who created all these? He who brings out the starry host one by one, and calls them each by name. Because of his great power and mighty strength, not one of them is missing.

Isaiah 40:26

The vastness of the universe continues to unfold to us through technological advances. The latest estimate for the number of stars is given as seven followed by twenty-two zeros. It is difficult to comprehend how large that number is. Scientists say it is about ten times the number of grains of sand on all the earth's beaches and deserts combined.[2] Next time you are at a beach, pick up a handful of sand and let it run through your fingers. Consider how many grains of sand there are on just one beach. Then try to imagine ten times the number of grains of sand on all the beaches and deserts in the world. The Lord Almighty, who made the unfathomable number of stars, wants to be your father. He promises to walk with you, live with you and receive you.

How are we to respond to these great promises? Twice in 2 Corinthians 6:16 - 7:1 we are told to purify ourselves. God wants us to purify ourselves from *everything* that contaminates us – *everything*. When we look at all the areas of our lives that we are called on to purify, this can seem like a daunting task. It was for me at first. I was overwhelmed as I contemplated all the ways I needed to purify myself. But I kept going and soon discovered something very powerful about purity: I was becoming a stronger person.

Before I began my study of purity, I did not understand the power of a pure life. If I needed more strength, I thought I should read the Bible more often or pray more (and I should). But we can pray, read the Bible, go to church and still be very weak Christians. Hopefully, doing these things will lead us to a closer walk with God, but the power of the scriptures comes as a result of faithfully putting them into practice (James 1:22-25).

After months of studying purity and seeing the connection between purity and strength, I awoke one morning feeling very discouraged. I was facing some rather big challenges, and was feeling that I could not get through the day. In my prayers that morning, I found myself asking God for strength. As those words crossed my lips, I realized I could do something about this – I could purify myself. So I began to consider what I might need to purify. In a quick moment, I realized I had some unrighteous attitudes toward another person, and impure and faithless thoughts going through my mind. These thoughts were taking a toll on me physically, emotionally and spiritually. So my prayers became much more specific, and with God's help, I began to purify my attitudes and thoughts. (We will look at this in detail in a later chapter.)

I was encouraged by the turnaround in my countenance. Rather than spending my day feeling discouraged and faithless, I experienced a wonderful day. I dealt with my impurity, and it had an immediate impact on my spirit. However, if I had gone through the day with a contaminated spirit, the outcome would have been very different. But that day I enjoyed the blessing of purifying my spirit.

* * *

As you begin this study on purity, I want to remind you that we should not pursue purity with legalism or self-righteousness. Both of these things can become big stumbling blocks. Legalism means that we follow a list of do's and don'ts. We can find ourselves doing things without getting our hearts involved. The Pharisees followed many rules and regulations, but Jesus said they were full of wickedness:

> *"Woe to you, teachers of the law and Pharisees, you hypocrites! You are like whitewashed tombs, which look beautiful on the outside but on the inside are full of dead men's bones and <u>everything unclean</u>. In the same way, on the outside you appear to people as righteous <u>but on the inside you are full of hypocrisy and wickedness</u>.* [Emphasis added.]
>
> Matthew 23:27-28

Even though they were very religious, they were living impure lives. On the outside, they appeared to be righteous, but God was just as concerned with what was going on in their hearts and minds as in their actions.

In addition to being legalistic, the Pharisees were also self-righteous. This too can become a stumbling block for us. Once we begin to purify our lives, it is tempting to start relying on ourselves more or to look down on other people who are not as *righteous* as we are. But we should never think we are righteous because of our own efforts. It is the blood of Jesus that purifies us:

> *But if we walk in the light, as he is in the light, we have fellowship with one another, and the blood of Jesus, his Son, <u>purifies us from all sin</u>.* [Emphasis added.]
>
> 1 John 1:7

We need to be humble as we purify ourselves, and remember that without Jesus' sacrifice, we would be unable to purify our lives and enjoy his blessings. This does not mean, however, that our purity is out of our control. Notice there is an "if" in this scripture – *if we walk in the light.* We still must do our part. In fact, the right response to God's forgiveness is to put our whole heart into purifying ourselves:

> *So then, dear friends, since you are looking forward to this, <u>make every effort to be found spotless</u>, blameless and at peace with him.* [Emphasis added.]
>
> 2 Peter 3:14

> *For you were once darkness, but now you are light in the Lord. Live as children of light (for the fruit of the light consists in all goodness, righteousness and truth) and <u>find out what pleases the Lord. Have nothing to do with the fruitless deeds of darkness</u>, but rather expose them.*
>
> Ephesians 5:8-11

> *Since we have these promises, dear friends, <u>let us purify ourselves from everything</u> that contaminates body and spirit, perfecting holiness out of reverence for God.*
>
> 2 Corinthians 7:1

These scriptures encourage us to respond aggressively by:

- making every effort,
- finding out what pleases the Lord,
- having nothing to do with deeds of darkness, and
- purifying ourselves from everything.

Note that the above scriptures were written to people who were already Christians. They were already forgiven of their sins, but were still being told to purify themselves from everything that contaminated them. As Christians we are called to make every effort as we purify ourselves. When we understand the blessings and benefits of purity, we see purity as a "get to," rather than a "have to." Just like enjoying pure water, spiritual purity is a great privilege.

Worksheet 1 - The Privilege of Purity

1. Do you equate spiritual purity with naïvety and vulnerability or with strength and honor? How do you perceive someone who is pure?

2. What do you think is the greatest appeal of spiritual purity?

3. In what ways do God's promises in connection with purity impact you?

4. Read 2 Corinthians 6:16 - 7:1. Meditate on God's greatness as you go through this day and remember his desire to be your Father. Consider also your response to this amazing offer and ways you can grow in your purity.

Memory Verse: 2 Corinthians 7:1

– Chapter 2 –

The Beauty of Purity

Not only is purity a privilege and a source of spiritual strength, it is also a great beautifier of the soul. In the next two chapters, we will explore the connection between purity and inner beauty. We will look at scriptures that give us some insight into spiritual beauty and how to become more beautiful to God. Then throughout this book, we will consider specific areas of purity that impact our inner beauty.

It is important to remember that God created beauty and our love for beautiful things is God-given. He created a marvelous world that can take our breath away:

> *He has made everything beautiful in its time . . .*
> Ecclesiastes 3:11

Beauty is a great motivator for us women. We not only enjoy beautiful things, we do crazy things to be a little more beautiful. We remove hair from our bodies with razors, wax or tweezers. We put smelly, dangerous chemicals on our hair. The labels warn us that these chemicals can cause blindness, but that does not stop us from using them. To be more beautiful, we deny ourselves favorite foods, wear uncomfortable shoes and make our bodies sweat. We do these things because beauty is empowering. We have all felt the confidence that a compliment brings or the deflation of looking at an unflattering photo of ourselves.

The relationship that we have with beauty is complex. It is powerful and inspiring, but also elusive and frustrating. A recent study, *The Real Truth about Beauty: A Global Report*, reported that only two percent of the women surveyed would describe themselves as beautiful. They also found that many women actually feel uncomfortable using the word "beautiful" to describe themselves. Sixty-seven percent of those surveyed chose "average" or "natural" to describe their appearance.[3]

This study stated that we see about 2,000 images per week of what the media defines as beautiful. But the media's definition of beauty is too narrow. *Webster's* defines beauty as the quality attributed to whatever pleases or satisfies the senses or mind, as by line, color, form, texture, proportion, rhythmic motion, tone, etc., or by behavior or attitude.[4]

We can experience beauty through all of our senses. The most obvious is by what we see, but beauty is also to be enjoyed through smell, taste, touch and sound. For example, the beauty of a rose is not only in how it looks, but also in its fragrance and smooth velvety petals. And the beauty of an elegantly displayed meal is enjoyed by sight, aroma and taste. We can also enjoy many beautiful sounds – a babbling brook, the singing of a song bird or the sound of a musical instrument. God created beauty to be enjoyed through each of our senses. Beauty is much broader than what we routinely see in the media.

The commercialization of beauty has influenced us in many ways. Even some of the most beautiful women do not feel beautiful. How do you feel about your beauty? Do you feel beautiful? Hopefully, you do, but if you don't, I have great news: spiritual beauty is for absolutely every one of us. And we don't want to think "average" when it comes to our spiritual beauty. This is a beauty in which each one of us can excel.

Have you ever thought about what your spirit looks like? If you got up tomorrow morning, looked into your mirror and all you could see was your spirit, what would your reflection reveal to you? The more I have studied spiritual beauty, the more intrigued I am by it. What does my spirit look like and how can I make myself more beautiful to

God? These are important questions because the only thing you get to take from this world is your soul. By making yourself more spiritually beautiful, you are preparing for the most important day of your life.

The following passage gives us insight into spiritual beauty:

> *Your adornment must not be merely external—braiding the hair, and wearing gold jewelry, or putting on dresses; but let it be the hidden person of the heart, with the imperishable quality of a gentle and quiet spirit, which is precious in the sight of God. For in this way in former times the holy women also, who hoped in God, used to adorn themselves . . .*
>
> 1 Peter 3:3-5 (NASB)

First of all, I would like to point out that this verse says, "Your adornment must not be *merely* external." Some have come to the conclusion that we should not make ourselves physically beautiful in order to enjoy spiritual beauty. This verse does not say that. It says we need to have *more* than external beauty.

We learn some very important aspects of inner beauty from this scripture. Most importantly, it is imperishable. (The New International Version says unfading). To understand how important this is, I encourage you to get two pictures of your mother (or grandmother), one when she was a young woman and the other as an old woman. Put them side by side and consider the fading nature of our external beauty. Then consider having a beauty that never fades. Keep these pictures handy as a daily reminder about the unfading nature of inner beauty.

We also learn that a gentle and quiet spirit is an important part of spiritual beauty. These qualities are perceived by many women as weak or passive qualities. However, the truth is that the original Greek text describes a strong and peaceful woman. The following excerpt from my book, *A Gentle & Quiet Spirit,* explains these qualities:

Gentle

The Greek word translated "gentle" or "meek" is *praus.*

Definition: *Praus* (prah-ooce´); the exercises of it are first toward God. It is that temper of spirit in which we

19

accept his dealings with us as good without disputing or resisting and is closely linked with the word humility. It is only the humble heart which is also *praus*, and which, as such, does not fight against God. *Praus* is the opposite of self-assertiveness and self-interest.

The meaning of *praus* is not easily expressed in English, for the terms gentleness and meekness, commonly used, suggest weakness, whereas *praus* does nothing of the kind. The common assumption is that when a man is meek or gentle, it is because he cannot help himself, but the Lord was *praus* because he had the infinite resources of God at his command.[5]

Praus means power under control, or power that is submitted or surrendered. It takes great inner strength to be *praus*. The English word "gentleness" refers more to actions, whereas *praus* refers more to a condition of mind and heart.[6] Our modern usage for "gentle" and "meek" is being mild or weak, lacking in spirit and courage. Having no inner strength and being easily imposed upon is how some people perceive a gentle and quiet spirit. Maybe that's how Pilate viewed Jesus when he made no reply (Matthew 27:13-14), but Jesus was not answering *because* he had inner strength.

Consider Jesus in the following verse, and imagine this taking place:

> *Say to the Daughter of Zion, "See, your king comes to you, gentle [praus] and riding on a donkey, on a colt, the foal of a donkey."*
>
> Matthew 21:5

Do you picture Jesus looking docile as he rode a donkey into Jerusalem? Read the definition of *praus* again and think about Jesus entering Jerusalem. When it says Jesus was *praus*, it is describing his attitude toward God. Jesus knew he was facing crucifixion, yet he was willing to go into Jerusalem. He was *praus*.

When Jesus was arrested, he said, "Do you think I cannot call on my Father, and he will at once put at my disposal more than twelve legions of angels?" (Matthew 26:53). A legion is an army of up to 5,000 men.[7] So Jesus is saying that he could have called more than 60,000 angels. One would have been enough! Jesus was gentle (*praus*) because he had incredible power at his disposal and he chose not to use it. Instead he submitted himself to God and made himself available for God's plan for his life.

When I studied the Greek word *praus* and found that it described a strong woman instead of a weak one, it drastically changed how I read this verse. I found it more appealing.

Quiet

The Greek word translated "quiet" is *hesuchios*.

> **Definition**: *Hesuchios* (hay-soo´-khee-os); tranquillity arising from within,[8] undisturbed and undisturbing, peaceable, and quiet.[9]

As a young child, I lived near a spring of water where my father would fill our water cans. Someone had put a concrete liner in the ground around the spring so that it was easy to draw the water out. I loved to go there. It was a peaceful place where water constantly bubbled up from within the earth and overflowed. It was puzzling to me how year after year the water kept coming. There was an invisible underground source that I could not understand as a child. I think of that spring every time I read this definition of "tranquillity arising from within." The quiet spirit also has an unseen source. It comes from a deep trust in God's love, protection and promises.

There are a lot of things we face every day that reveal whether or not we have this kind of spirit. Does "tranquillity arising from within" describe you or would "stressed-out" be a better fit? Stress, not tranquillity, describes many women today. Think back on what the last week was like for you and your household. Were you undisturbed by the events you faced and undisturbing to others around you? Did you raise your voice or somehow lose control? Were you peaceful in the middle of all your busyness? Now, I assume you have been busy. I am not talking about whether or not you have a life of leisure. I am talking about an inner quality.

Again, Jesus is the perfect example of *hesuchios*. Large crowds of people who were needy, hungry and sick often surrounded him (sounds like a family at times). Luke 8:42 says, "As Jesus was on his way, the crowds almost crushed him." It goes on to say that a woman touched him and that Jesus took the time to inquire about it. Unlike his disciples, who urged Jesus to send needy people away (Mark 6:36), Jesus was unruffled by the crowds. We also read about him sleeping in a boat during a storm. You can see his incredible peace and his trust in God as he deals with his disciples' fear (Matthew 8:23-26). Jesus completely trusted God:

> *For I did not speak of my own accord, but the Father who sent me commanded me what to say and how to say it. I know that his command leads to eternal life. So whatever I say is just what the Father has told me to say.*
>
> John 12:49-50

He knew that God's commands would lead him to eternal life, in other words, get him back to heaven. He trusted God completely, including what to say and how to say it. What a remarkable level of trust!

There are many scriptures that give us direction on what to say and not say and how to say it and not say it. It is my goal to trust God completely, but occasionally my lack of tranquillity shows me that I am not. When I am in a stressful situation is when I am most apt to say and do things that I later regret. At these times, I can usually find that I am not trusting God about something. Consider the following scriptures:

> *May the God of hope fill you with all joy and peace as you* <u>*trust in him,*</u> *so that you may overflow with hope by the power of the Holy Spirit.* [Emphasis added.]
>
> Romans 15:13

> <u>*Trust in him at all times,*</u> *O people; pour out your hearts to him, for God is our refuge.* [Emphasis added.]
>
> Psalms 62:8

> *Do not let your hearts be troubled.* <u>*Trust in God;*</u> <u>*trust also in me.*</u> [Emphasis added.]
>
> John 14:1

Notice in these verses how trust is connected to joy, peace, and refuge. The quiet spirit (tranquility arising from within) is not a fluff quality. It comes from a deep trust in God's love, protection and promises.

A woman with a gentle and quiet spirit is an amazing woman. She is a woman with great inner strength, who has a close relationship with God. She trusts God to direct her, and she is overflowing with peace. She is both *praus* and *hesuchios*.[10]

* * *

Can you imagine how God must feel about a woman with a gentle and quiet spirit? She is so surrendered to him that she is overflowing with tranquility. This helps us understand God's great appreciation of these qualities:

> *Instead, it should be that of your inner self, the unfading beauty of a gentle and quiet spirit, which is of* <u>*great worth in God's sight.*</u> [Emphasis added.]
>
> 1 Peter 3:4

The following is another excerpt from *A Gentle & Quiet Spirit* which explains how much God values this inner beauty.

Great Worth

Can you imagine something being valuable to God? He is the creator. Doesn't he have everything? We read in the Bible that he doesn't need anything (Acts 17:25); however, 1 Peter 3:4 says that there is something that is of great worth to him. The Greek word translated "great worth" is *poluteles*.

Definition: *Poluteles* (pol-oo-tel-ace); the very end or limit with reference to price; of the highest cost, very expensive, very precious.[11]

Poluteles means the *very* end or limit. In other words, this is at the top of God's list of what he considers most precious to him. What do you think God values? Is a gentle and quiet spirit something that you would have listed as one of the things that is highly valued by God?

What do you value the most? I have a diamond engagement ring that I cherish. I treat it with great care because of its value and its sentimental significance. I have many other things I value and protect, but they are not at the top of my list. My family tops my list. I would give up my life for them. They are priceless to me.

Sometimes it is not clear what we mean by the word "great." If you are single and I set you up on a blind date and told you that this guy is great, you might ask me some questions: "What's great about him?" Or, "How great is 'great'?"

We often use the word "great" in a casual way. We might say that it is a great day, but we are only casually comparing the last few days. However, God is not saying "great" casually. *Poluteles* means the very end or limit with reference to value. This Greek word is also used in Mark 14:3-5.

> . . . *a woman came with an alabaster jar of very expensive [poluteles] perfume, made of pure nard. She broke the jar and poured the perfume on his head . . . It could have been sold for more than a year's wages . . .*
>
> Mark 14:3-5

This passage gives us more insight into the word *poluteles*. This perfume was worth more than a year's salary. Personally, I've never spent more than half of one day's wages for perfume. Most perfumes today cost between $25 and $100. The most expensive perfume that I've ever seen cost $400 an ounce. But even that perfume would not be close in comparison to a perfume that cost more than a year's salary.

If you had a bottle of perfume that cost more than what you make in a year (or could make), how would you take care of it compared to your other perfumes? And how would you describe it compared to your other perfumes? I probably would repeat the word "very" several times just so that it is clear how valuable it is – *very, very, very* expensive perfume. When you compare the perfume that was poured on Jesus with any other perfume, nothing comes close.

When God says *poluteles* in 1 Peter 3:4, he means *great* worth or *very* precious. This tops his list. A gentle and quiet spirit is of great worth to him.[12]

* * *

It can be difficult to accept how much God values these qualities, especially if you do not understand them and have not valued them much yourself. But the truth is that these are beautiful qualities, and they are highly valued by God.

* * *

At the beginning of this chapter, I said we would explore the connection between purity and inner beauty. Let's look again at the following verse:

> Since we have these promises, dear friends, let us purify ourselves from everything that contaminates [molusmos] body and spirit, perfecting holiness out of reverence for God.
>
> 2 Corinthians 7:1

The Greek word translated "contaminates" is *molusmos*.

Definition: *Molusmos* (mol-oos-mos); a stain or filthiness.[13]

Stains, filthiness and contamination give us a good picture of the inner ugliness that we must fight in order to become more spiritually beautiful. Understanding how to purify these things from our spirits is the first step to real spiritual beauty.

Contamination just sounds bad, doesn't it? We do not want to be around anything that is contaminated. If we are, we want to know how to avoid it or what we must do to get rid of it. Even stains are a big deterrent when it comes to what we want to wear. I've been so embarrassed by a stained garment that I have discarded it. It was a perfectly good garment in every way except it had an unfortunate stain.

A stained garment can put an end to an outing. Recently when I was in an elevator at a shopping center, a woman walked into the elevator talking to me as if she knew me. She warned me about making sure the tops of my coffee cups were fastened correctly. She pointed to her clothing which was stained with coffee. She was so embarrassed that her shopping trip was over – she was going home to change her clothing.

Unlike a stained garment, however, we can remove our spiritual stains and purify ourselves from the filthiness we find in our lives. We can become more and more beautiful as we go through our lives.

Throughout this book, we will consider some of the spiritual stains we may find and consider how we can transform our inner *ugliness* into inner beauty. In the next chapter, we will consider how we can begin to explore our own inner beauty and what it takes to grow more and more beautiful to God.

Worksheet 2 - The Beauty of Purity

1. How would you describe a spiritually beautiful woman?

2. In what ways would surrendering more fully to God impact your inner beauty?

3. How would having a more tranquil spirit impact your inner beauty?

Memory Verse: Proverbs 31:30

– Chapter 3 –

Spiritual Adornment

For in this way in former times the holy women also, who hoped in God, used to adorn themselves. . .

1 Peter 3:5 (NASB)

Adornment is as natural to us as our love of beauty. I imagine Eve wore a necklace before she wore clothing. We get excited about rocks! Think about it. They are beautiful, but they are rocks! We can decorate just about every part of our bodies from the top of our heads to the tip of our toes. And there are beauty treatments for almost every inch of our bodies: hair coloring and styling, facials, make-up, manicures, pedicures, body waxing, tanning, body piercing, surgical enhancements and on and on. There are more beauty treatments than we can afford or have time for.

Every woman I know takes time to improve her looks. Some spend more time than others, but they all make beauty a priority. But what about our spiritual beauty? How do we begin to adorn ourselves spiritually? When I want to improve my physical beauty, I first go stand in front of a mirror and evaluate myself. This is also true for spiritual beauty. We first need to look into the spiritual mirror.

> *Do not merely listen to the word, and so deceive yourselves. Do what it says. Anyone who listens to the word but does not do what it says is like a man who looks at his face in a mirror and, after looking at himself, goes away and immediately*

forgets what he looks like. But the man who looks intently into the perfect law that gives freedom, and continues to do this, not forgetting what he has heard, but doing it--he will be blessed in what he does.

James 1:22-25

We have been given a spiritual mirror, and we need to look at it closely. That mirror is the Bible. Hebrews 4:12 says that God's word judges the thoughts and attitudes of the heart. The Bible can reflect back to us our deepest thoughts and attitudes, and it will help us judge whether they are good or bad. It can reveal to us things that will change us forever, and help us be prepared for the most important day of our lives.

How blessed we are to live during a time when Bibles are so readily available. If you need to purchase a Bible, you can find a selection in almost any store that sells books. You get to choose color and size, as well as paperback, hardbound or leather. But this has not always been the case. Not too many centuries ago, obtaining a Bible was a dangerous activity. For many years the Roman Catholic Church and the world leaders under its domain kept the scriptures from the common people. In fact, they threatened anyone possessing a non-Latin Bible with execution. They were hanged, drowned, torn in pieces or burned alive at the stake.

In the 1380s, John Wycliffe, an Oxford professor, produced the first hand-written English language Bible manuscripts. With the help of faithful scribes, he produced dozens of English language manuscripts of the Bible. The Pope was so infuriated by his teachings and his translation of the Bible into English that forty-four years after Wycliffe's death, he ordered that Wycliffe's bones be dug up, crushed and scattered in the river! That made no difference to Wycliffe, but it was the beginning of a great battle over whether or not common people could read the Bible in their own language.

In the 1490s, Thomas Linacre, another Oxford professor and the personal physician to King Henry VII and King Henry VIII, decided to learn Greek. After reading the Gospels in Greek and comparing it to the Latin Vulgate, he wrote in his diary, "Either this (the original

Greek) is not the Gospel . . . or we are not Christians." The Latin had become so corrupt that it no longer even preserved the message of the Gospel, yet the Church still threatened to kill anyone who read the scripture in any language other than Latin.

It was a turbulent time for the reformers. According to Foxe's Book of Martyrs, in 1517, seven people were burned at the stake by the Roman Catholic Church for the crime of teaching their children the Lord's prayer in English rather than Latin.

The printing press was invented in the 1450s, and the first book to ever be printed was a Latin language Bible. By the early 1500s, Martin Luther and William Tyndale were printing copies of the New Testament which they'd translated into German and English, respectively, from the original Greek text. Tyndale's copies of the New Testament made their way into England despite the efforts of King Henry VIII to confiscate them. Tyndale was eventually burned at the stake in 1536. Ironically, three years later, King Henry VIII allowed, and even funded, the printing of the English Bible in defiance of the Pope. The King had asked the Pope to grant him a divorce so that he could marry his mistress. When the Pope refused, the King responded by separating himself from the Catholic Church and starting the Anglican Church, also known as the Church of England.

However this battle was still not over. Later when Queen "Bloody" Mary took the throne, she wanted to reunite with the Catholic Church, and again made it illegal to own a non-Latin Bible.[14]

During this period in history, many people gave their lives for the privilege of reading the Bible. Today we do not fear being put to death for reading the Bible, but Satan still has many schemes to keep us from embracing God's word. The following story illustrates one of them:

> As Jesus and his disciples were on their way, he came to a village where a woman named Martha opened her home to him. She had a sister called Mary, who sat at the Lord's feet listening to what he said. But Martha was distracted by all the preparations that had to be made. She came to him and asked, "Lord, don't you care that my sister has left me to do the work by myself? Tell her to help me!"

31

> *"Martha, Martha,"* the Lord answered, *"you are worried and upset about many things, but only one thing is needed. Mary has chosen what is better, and it will not be taken away from her."*

Luke 10:38-42

Most of us know this story and relate well to it. The pressures of Martha's life pulled her away from her time with Jesus. This resulted in her being upset with Mary for not helping her with chores, and with Jesus for not seeming to care. She needed Jesus to help her see the truth about herself because her own spiritual condition was not obvious to her. She needed her spiritual mirror.

The Christians mentioned in the following scripture also had a distorted view of their true spiritual condition:

> *You say, "I am rich; I have acquired wealth and do not need a thing." But you do not realize that you are wretched, pitiful, poor, blind and naked.*

Revelation 3:17

This must have been a shock to hear. They thought they were doing well, but Jesus told them they were actually very needy. How embarrassing! This is one of the challenges we also face when looking into a mirror – it may show us something that we would rather not see.

I have been embarrassed this way. Many years ago, when my sons were preschoolers, I babysat for three women in my neighborhood. One morning I overslept and had to rush to get ready for their arrival. I quickly glanced into a mirror as I headed to the kitchen to start cooking breakfast. I was shocked by what I saw. The night before I had been over-zealous in my use of an acne product for my face. I had dried spots all over my face. I intended to return and clean my face, but I forgot. It was just like James 1:24 that describes someone who, "after looking at himself, goes away and *immediately* forgets what he looks like." The three women, looking very professional, dropped off their children, and a few minutes after the last one had left, I happened to walk past the mirror again. I was so embarrassed! Today I think it's funny, but I was more horrified than amused back then. They had seen a side of me I did not want revealed.

We can feel the same way about our spiritual flaws. If we study the Bible, our spiritual flaws will be revealed. As a result, we may be tempted to avoid the spiritual mirror. But that does not make sense. It would not have helped me to avoid a mirror for the rest of that day – I still had the spots on my face. Don't let a fear of the truth keep you from looking into this amazing spiritual mirror. It will guide you and help you become more spiritually beautiful. And remember that James 1:25 says we will be blessed by looking intently into God's law if we will put it into practice.

Another thing to consider about a mirror is that it is a time of self-reflection. It is not a time to consider how someone else looks, but a time to consider your own reflection. I don't get up in the morning, go stand before my mirror and think, "I've seen so-and-so's hair look a lot worse than mine!" No, I think, "My hair is a mess! I've got to wash it." I am there to evaluate my own issues. When I am reading my Bible, it is a time to let the scriptures reflect back the things I need to see about myself and the ways that I can make myself more beautiful to God.

This is doubly important if you study the Bible to prepare lessons that you will teach, or if you study the Bible with other women to help them understand the scriptures. This should not be the full extent of your personal study. That would be like a beautician who helps other women look more beautiful but never styles her own hair. We need to come before our spiritual mirror every day to evaluate our own hearts before God. What a shame it would be to help other women be beautiful before God and not personally enjoy spiritual beauty each day.

Another mirror analogy that I'd like to consider is the use of a second mirror. When I want to check the back of my hair, I take my small hand mirror, turn around and look into the small mirror so I can see the back of my hair in my big mirror. Or when I'm trying on a new outfit at a dress shop, I will stand in front of a three-way mirror so I can see how this outfit looks all the way around. A second or third mirror helps me get a perspective that one mirror can't give me. As much as I try, I cannot get a complete picture by using only one mirror. The same is true of my spiritual mirror. That second mirror is like the discipleship of an honest Christian sister who will help me see things in my life that I do not see. Discipleship helps me to see a more complete view of myself.

We must look intently into God's word. It will strengthen us and bring us closer to God. It will guide us as we consider how to grow in our spiritual beauty and how to fight the battle for greater purity. Keep your spiritual mirror close and look into it often.

Looking into the spiritual mirror is only the beginning. The next step is to take action. The first place to begin is to consider your spiritual clothing. Many scriptures describe aspects of spiritual clothing. 2 Corinthians 5:3 says that when we are clothed, we will not be found naked. Our spiritual clothing is as important for our spirits as our physical clothing is for our bodies.

> ... for all of you who were baptized into Christ have clothed yourselves with Christ.
>
> Galatians 3:27

The most important spiritual garment we can clothe ourselves with is Christ.

* * *

> She is clothed with strength and dignity; she can laugh at the days to come.
>
> Proverbs 31:25

Would you like to wear strength and dignity? Both of these qualities give us confidence. Maybe that is why she can laugh at the days to come. It was reported in *The Real Truth About Beauty* that 86% percent of the women surveyed agreed that happiness is the primary element in making a woman beautiful, and they themselves feel most beautiful when they are happy and fulfilled in their lives.[15]

* * *

> Awake, awake, O Zion, clothe yourself with strength. Put on your garments of splendor, O Jerusalem, the holy city...
>
> Isaiah 52:1

This is another reference to strength. It also mentions garments of splendor. You can be dressed up spiritually, not just physically.

* * *

...bestow on them a crown of beauty instead of ashes, the oil of gladness instead of mourning, and a garment of praise instead of a spirit of despair ...

Isaiah 61:3

This verse paints a striking contrast. Do you want to wear a beautiful crown or ashes on your head? Do you want to be happy or sad? Do you want to be filled with praise or despair? These are easy questions to answer!

* * *

For this is the way the holy women of the past who put their hope in God used to make themselves beautiful. They were submissive to their own husbands.

1 Peter 3:5

Submission is also an adorning quality. This is how holy women make themselves beautiful.

* * *

Therefore, as God's chosen people, holy and dearly loved, clothe yourselves with compassion, kindness, humility, gentleness and patience.

Colossians 3:12

Kindness, compassion, humility, gentleness and patience are qualities of spiritual beauty. Tabitha was known for abounding with deeds of "kindness and charity" (Acts 9:36 NASB). We are not told what she looked like, but we know her spirit was beautifully clothed.

* * *

Good deeds are also part of our spiritual adornment:

I also want women to dress modestly, with decency and propriety, not with braided hair or gold or pearls or expensive clothes, but with good deeds, appropriate for women who profess to worship God. [Emphasis added.]

1 Timothy 2:9-10

This scripture gives us insight into spiritual adornment, but it also raises a question. Does this scripture mean that we can't wear gold, pearls, braided hair or expensive clothing? If we take it literally, we are to wear good deeds. How modest would that be? Consider too that not wearing gold or not braiding your hair will not necessarily make you a more godly woman. This verse is not meant to create a dress code. As Christians, we have many freedoms in Christ. Yet, there are some important guidelines about modesty and decency in this scripture. And there is also a very important principle of true beauty that we must understand: **Your godly actions are more adorning than stylish hair, beautiful jewelry or expensive clothing!**

1 Peter 3:3-4 also makes a similar comparison of physical adornment to spiritual qualities:

> *Your adornment must not be merely external—braiding the hair, and wearing gold jewelry, or putting on dresses; but let it be the hidden person of the heart . . .*
>
> 1 Peter 3:3-4 (NASB)

Some of the most beautiful things we can wear are gold and jewels. But do these things really make us more beautiful? I believe most women would answer yes to that question. Personally, I like a little sparkle on my ears! I think it spiffs me up a little. The point of these scriptures is that godliness is by far more beautifying than these lovely things with which we adorn ourselves.

We know how to improve our physical beauty, and we go to great lengths and expense to do so. But as women who profess to worship God, our beauty must go much deeper than what we adorn ourselves with on the outside. We must also adorn ourselves on the inside with spiritual qualities. In the long run, it is our spiritual beauty that really matters:

> *. . . beauty is fleeting, but a woman who fears the Lord is to be praised.*
>
> Proverbs 31:30

I want to emphasize that looking bad on the outside is not the goal. That won't make you look more beautiful on the inside. We can enjoy our physical beauty, but in the end, our inner beauty will be of far greater importance.

Some of the holy women in the Bible were known for their physical beauty as well as their spiritual beauty. Sarah must have been very beautiful. She was twice taken from Abraham by kings. The second time was after Abraham mentioned that she was ninety years old (Genesis 17:17; 20:2). Ninety years old and still beautiful! Esther must have also been especially beautiful. And she was not only beautiful, she was pampered. She spent a year in beauty treatments and won the beauty contest to be queen. However, it is Sarah's and Esther's spiritual beauty that lives on. It is imperishable. They trusted God and surrendered their lives to his will.

Inner beauty is a powerful force. A pagan named Libanius (314-394 A.D.), who was an educated Greek-speaking teacher, is said to have exclaimed in admiration and astonishment, "What women these Christians have!"[16] I wonder why Libanius was so impressed by them? Was it their courage? Perhaps it was their purity, happiness or contentment. What do you think impresses a man? Is he more impressed by jewelry or actions? Personally, I don't think it's our jewelry. Women are much more interested in jewelry than men. My husband is more impressed by my happiness than a beautiful piece of jewelry I might happen to be wearing. He loves it when I'm happy.

Happiness is a great beautifier of both body and spirit. Conduct a test the next time you're getting dressed up. After you have done everything to look your very best, stand in front of a mirror and put anger on your face. How does that make you look? Then put joy on your face. Or try putting fear or worry on your face, then melt it away with peacefulness. Isn't that the quickest beauty treatment you have ever seen? (I'm serious. Do this. It may seem a little crazy, but it will give you deeper convictions about inner beauty.)

I have seen women grow in their beauty when they became Christians. Faithful Christian women are some of the most beautiful women I know. As they purified their lives, they overcame fear, anger, worry, hatred, and so forth. This is an inner beauty that shows through – a beauty that no spa treatment can bring about. It is a beauty that comes from a faithful and contented life.

* * *

I want to encourage you to wear your beautiful spiritual garments every day and consider how to spiritually adorn yourself. Don't settle for only the outward. Take the time to consider your inner beauty and what makes you beautiful forever.

Worksheet 3 - Spiritual Adornment

1. What is your greatest challenge in having consistent and meaningful Bible studies?

2. Are you more serious about your inward beauty or your outward beauty?

3. What is your reaction to stains on a garment? Are you as concerned about spiritual stains?

4. What are your favorite ways to adorn yourself physically?

5. What qualities make you feel spiritually beautiful?

Memory Verse: 1 Peter 3:3-4

– Chapter 4 –

Modesty and Decorum

In the last chapter, we considered our spiritual "clothing" and how we can adorn ourselves spiritually. Let's now consider our physical clothing and how that might reflect upon our purity.

> *I also want women to dress modestly, with decency . . .*
> 1 Timothy 2:9

We have been given some basic biblical guidelines concerning our clothing. Clothing is mentioned as far back as Adam and Eve. After Adam and Eve disobeyed God, their first response was to hide because of their nakedness. They felt ashamed without clothing, so God made garments for them before he sent them out of the Garden of Eden (Genesis 3:21). Clothing, or a lack of it, is mentioned in many stories in the Bible. Examples include Noah's nakedness and the impact it had on his family (Genesis 9:21-25); Rebekah deceiving Isaac by having Jacob put on his brother's clothes (Genesis 27:15); Tamar dressing like a prostitute to deceive her father-in-law (Genesis 38:13-15); and John the Baptist's unusual choice of clothing (Matthew 3:4).

The clothing we choose to wear or not wear says a lot about us. We can actually make a statement by what we wear. If a woman arrived at a social event wearing a pantsuit, button-down shirt, tie and wingtip shoes, she would be making a strong anti-feminine statement. An all leather outfit would make a different statement, or a lacy blouse and ruffled skirt would make yet another statement.

Fashion is a multi-billion dollar industry, and it is always changing. It is to the designers' financial benefit to change the styles. It keeps them in business. As long as I can remember, there have been do's and don'ts about the latest styles, such as whether pleats are "in" or pleats are "out"; whether pink is popular or passé. And don't forget the old standby rules of fashion, such as don't wear white shoes before Memorial Day or after Labor Day, or just don't wear white shoes at all. Fashion rules are ever-changing, but what about the never-changing scriptures? What do they say about our fashion choices?

> *I also want women to dress modestly [kosmois], with decency [aidos]...*
>
> 1 Timothy 2:9

The Greek word translated "modestly" is *kosmois*.

Definition: *Kosmios* (kos´-mee-os); orderly, i.e., decorous: of good behavior, modest.[17]

Modest means having or showing a moderate opinion of one's own value, abilities, achievements; not forward; behaving, dressing or speaking in a way that is considered proper or decorous; decent; moderate or reasonable; not extreme; quiet and humble in appearance, style; not pretentious.[18]

1 Timothy 2:9 uses two different words that have to do with modesty. The first one is *kosmios*, which is translated as modestly, and the second one is *aidos* which is translated as decency. Both words have to do with modesty, but *aidos* is more about a sense of shame or decency. (We will look at *aidos* in the next chapter.) *Kosmios* has to do with modesty or decorum.

Decorous or decorum means good taste in behavior, speech, or dress; an act or requirement of polite behavior.[19] For example, how would you feel if you were a bride and one of your bridesmaids wore blue jeans to your wedding instead of the dress you selected for her? Or if you hired someone to represent your business to the public, how would you feel if they showed up for work wearing wrinkled, dirty clothing? Proper decorum is one way to show respect and honor to other people.

Decorum simply means showing consideration for others. We can do that by what we wear. Not that we are dressing to impress, but we can dress in a way that is polite and considerate of others. When our fashion becomes all about us, we are missing an important aspect of being a Christian.

Generally, there is a stronger sense of decorum with regard to weddings and funerals than most events. But there are numerous other times we need to make sure we are considerate in what we wear. Today many associate decorum with stiffness (uncoolness) or formality. Over the last several decades, our culture has become so casual that proper decorum is often ridiculed. In the 1970s, an anti-establishment theme that was popular was "do your own thing." It's a theme that has permeated our culture. Yet, 1 Timothy 2:9-10 calls us to be considerate of others in our choice of clothing.

What would "modest" or "decorous" look like for Christian women today? It would certainly be different from one-hundred years ago, and much different from two-hundred years ago. It's a moving standard. Since it's a moving standard, can we just do our own thing? Is decorum really necessary? The Bible can help us with this. There are many verses about being considerate of others. Consider the following scriptures in light of your choice of clothing:

> *Do nothing out of selfish ambition or vain conceit, but in humility consider others better than yourselves.*
>
> Philippians 2:3

> *For we are taking pains to do what is right, not only in the eyes of the Lord but also in the eyes of men.*
>
> 2 Corinthians 8:21

> *Be devoted to one another in brotherly love. Honor one another above yourselves.*
>
> Romans 12:10

I'm not suggesting that we must closely follow Emily Post's book on proper etiquette. However, there are many opportunities for us to show consideration to those around us. One of them is by the way we dress. That's the point of 1 Timothy 2:9 when it says to dress in a decorous or modest way. As our clothing reflects our personalities, it should also reflect our consideration for others. This is one of our spiritual beauty treatments – consideration for others.

Worksheet 4 - Modesty & Decorum

1. When are times that you show others consideration through your choices?

_____

_____

_____

2. Do you see decorum as politeness or stiffness? Why?

_____

_____

_____

3. How does considering others impact our spiritual beauty?

_____

_____

_____

4. Do you have a strong consideration for other people when it comes to your choices? Is there an area in which you need to grow?

_____

_____

_____

_____

_____

_____

_____

Memory Verse: Philippians 2:3

– Chapter 5 –

Decency and Propriety

I also want women to dress modestly, with decency [aidos] and propriety [sophrosyne] . . .

1 Timothy 2:9

The Greek word translated "decency" is *aidos*.

Definition: *Aidos* (ahee-doce´); a sense of shame or modesty. Shamefastness is modesty which is "fast" or rooted in the character. *Aidos* would always restrain a good man from an unworthy act.[20]

The word *aidos* means having a strong sense of shame. (Shame is a painful feeling of having lost the respect of others.[21]) The word "shamefastness" is a little archaic. Shame-fast-ness would mean you keep it close to you. However, women today are taught the opposite of this concept. We are taught to be bold and never feel ashamed of anything, as though there were something inherently wrong with shame. Sadly, there is misdirected shame that some people bear, but shame, in and of itself, is not always bad.

Shame is an interesting emotion. It is a painful emotion, but it has a spiritual purpose. It is like an alarm that warns us that we are moving away from the godly principles that will protect us. The danger is that we harden our hearts and ignore the warning:

Are they ashamed of their loathsome conduct? No, they have no shame at all; they do not even know how to blush. So they will

fall among the fallen; they will be brought down when they are punished, says the LORD.
                                                                    Jeremiah 8:12

We don't want to unduly feel shame, but we need to feel it if we are out of line with God. Forgetting how to blush can be a gradual process over several years; a process in which we finally get to a point of accepting things that are immodest or indecent. For example, women wear clothing today that, a decade ago, they would not have considered wearing outside their bedrooms. Now it is a common practice.

Discretion is a quality that will help us navigate the maze of choices offered by the fashion world, and use good judgment about what we wear. It helps us see the bigger picture of the physical and spiritual choices before us. Consider what the Bible has to say about discretion:

Discretion will protect you, and understanding will guard you.
                                                                    Proverbs 2:11

Like a gold ring in a pig's snout is a beautiful woman who shows no discretion.
                                                                    Proverbs 11:22

Picture a pig with a gold snout ring. What a disgusting and ugly picture! Without discretion, that's how our spirits looks. Discretion will protect us and help us become more spiritually beautiful.

The Greek word translated "propriety" in 1 Timothy 2:9 is *sophrosyne.*

Definition: *Sophrosyne* (so-fros-oo´-nay); sound judgment. It is that habitual inner self-government, with its constant rein on all passions and desires, enabling the believer to be conformed to the mind of Christ. Its root word is *sophrono* which is translated soberminded or safe or sound in mind; moderate as to opinion or passion; discreet, temperate.[22]

Propriety is a word we don't use much today, and many would have a difficult time defining it. Propriety means the quality of being proper or to conform to what is proper.[23] However, this gives an incomplete picture of what the Greek word *sophrosyne* means. Although *sophrosyne* leads you to do what is proper, it has a much deeper meaning. It has to do with what you allow yourself to think about – having a constant rein on your desires and passions. And this is self-government, not a pressure from others to conform.

With *sophrosyne* you can turn your thoughts away from things that might be harmful to you; things such as worry, self-hatred or jealousy. With a "constant rein on all passions and desires," you can control an angry thought and not say something improper. On the outside you may have done what was proper, but you were using restraint on a much deeper level. *Sophrosyne* is essential as you choose your clothing. Is it decent? Is this something a godly woman would wear, or am I being caught up in *fashionable* indecency?

Who started the latest styles anyway? Was it a godly woman or a worldly woman? Who are you following in your fashion choices? Sound judgment is what we need to help us think through our choices of fashion. It will help us when we think about wearing something we should not wear. And sound judgment will help us as we look at areas where the decisions we face are more difficult. For example, we can find comfort in our clothes because they are not on the edge of fashion. But we fail to realize that the edge of what is fashionable may have moved far beyond what is decent. We need sound judgment when it comes to deciding if we will wear the latest fashions.

The Trickle-Up Effect

The trickle-down effect is a term most often associated with economics, but it is also used in the world of fashion. In fashion, the term refers to a theory that when the lowest social class, or a perceived lower social class, adopts a particular fashion, that fashion is no longer desirable to the leaders in the highest social class.[24]

It makes sense that things trickle down, whether it is economics or fashion. But did you know that there is a phenomenon in the fashion world that can be called the trickle-up effect? Let me explain. My mom, who was married at the age of 20 in 1945, tells me that once she was married, she did her best to look older. It was common practice for young married women to try to look more matronly.

When I was in high school in the late 1960s, being skinny was unattractive. I was 5'6" at the time and weighed 105 pounds, and I received a great deal of teasing about my weight. I did everything I could to gain weight but to no avail. A few years later, when I took my first job as a court reporter for a district judge, I was teased about looking like a teenager. Even at the age of 28, when I was married and had two small children, I would have door-to-door salesmen ask me if my mom was at home. I once replied, "My mom does not live here." He then asked to speak with my dad. I so wanted to look like a "woman." It took me years to work through my dislike for my skinny and youthful body. This may sound strange today, but that was how I thought about my skinny and youthful appearance.

Fast forward four decades to today. Women of all ages are obsessed with looking younger, thinner and sexier. Fashions designed for older women look more and more like the fashions worn by young women. That's the trickle-up effect – older women now want to dress like young women, rather than young girls wanting to dress like their moms.

I just shake my head when I think how some young girls starve themselves because they want to be thinner. Times have certainly changed! But why? How has this drastic change come about? How have we gone from icons like Marilyn Monroe to the skinny supermodels of today? The answer is that this is a by-product of the sexualization of young women through the media over the last several decades.

This focus on youth and sexiness has taken a significant toll on women of all ages. It is more obvious in the youth of today, but the sexualization of young women has impacted older women too. Older women now dress to look younger, thinner and sexier. Health services around the country are reporting an increase in the number of eating disorders in older women.[25] And fashions for older women are very youthful and sexy. Sometimes I find it very challenging to find modest clothing.

The roots of this problem are deep in our culture. The fashion world has not just suddenly decided to offer sexy clothing in the last few years. This trend has developed for decades through the media, and is now a part of our popular culture. Understanding how the sexualization of young women has created issues for all of us will help us make better judgements about what we will wear. This is another area that *sophrosyne* will help us be discreet in our fashion choices.

Sexy vs. Beautiful

I want to stress that dressing decently does not mean you have to wear ugly clothing or look matronly. We can wear beautiful (or stylish) clothing without dressing in an inappropriate way. Are you discreet about when to look sexy? If you are married, when do you dress the most seductively? Is it around your husband? Do you dress in a sexy way for dates with your husband? How about what you wear around the house or your sleepwear? You have it backwards if you dress sexy for work or when you are out with your girlfriends, but mostly wear sweats around your husband.

It is important to understand that men are sexually stimulated by what they see, and women are stimulated more through their emotions. Christian men have to learn to look away from a woman who is dressed in a sexy or provocative way. If your clothing is indecent, you can become an obstacle for a godly man. You are also an obstacle for an ungodly man, but he will look at you anyway. *Sophrosyne* will help us dress appropriately for the occasion and help us be considerate of others.

> *We put no stumbling block in anyone's path, so that our ministry will not be discredited. Rather, as servants of God we commend ourselves in every way . . . in purity . . .*
> 2 Corinthians 6:3-6

As servants of God, we must make sure we are not creating a stumbling block by the way we dress. Is your clothing decent? On a typical day, if a Christian man looked at you, would he need to look away to keep from being tempted? I've heard women say, "It's his problem, not mine." But that is not what the scriptures teach. The scriptures teach us to set an example in purity (1 Timothy 4:12), and to live a pure life that is commendable. Can you be commended for your discretion and decency?

51

You may be wondering, "Does it really matter?" "Is this really worthy of our consideration?" Yes to both questions!

> *"Woe to the world because of the things that cause people to sin! Such things must come, but woe to the man through whom they come! If your hand or your foot causes you to sin cut it off and throw it away. It is better for you to enter life maimed or crippled than to have two hands or two feet and be thrown into eternal fire. And if your eye causes you to sin, gouge it out and throw it away. It is better for you to enter life with one eye than to have two eyes and be thrown into the fire of hell."*
>
> Matthew 18:7-9

This scripture explains that we have a responsibility to those around us. We should take a radical approach to things that will cause us or someone else to sin. About fifteen years ago, a young single mom began studying the Bible and soon became a Christian. As her convictions grew through her studies, she realized she did not dress in a modest way. She went home and sifted through her clothes. As she was sorting them, she decided to throw away anything that was indecent because she did not want to encourage anyone else to wear it. Today she is a beautiful woman who is known for her godly life. She took a radical approach to her modesty, and God has blessed her life in many ways.

I want to stress that I'm not saying you should wear dowdy, unflattering clothing. Dress beautifully, but remember that your outward beauty is nothing in comparison to your inner beauty. Use discretion as you make your choices. It is one of our greatest spiritual beauty treatments.

Worksheet 5 - Decency and Propriety

1. Do you have a strong sense of decency when it comes to your clothing?

2. Who influences your fashion choices the most?

3. Do you wear clothing today that you would have considered immodest five or ten years ago?

4. If you are married, when and where do you wear your sexiest clothing?

Memory Verse: Proverbs 11:22

– Chapter 6 –

Motives of the Heart

All a man's ways seem innocent to him, but motives are weighed by the LORD.

Proverbs 16:2

Therefore judge nothing before the appointed time; wait till the Lord comes. He will bring to light what is hidden in darkness and will expose the motives of men's hearts. At that time each will receive his praise from God.

1 Corinthians 4:5

Our motives count before God, so it's important for us to consider the "why" behind our choices. In the previous chapter, we looked at the Greek word *sophrosyne*, which is translated as propriety. Propriety *(sophrosyne)* will help us more than simply deciding whether something is decent; it will help us with the deeper issue of why we would want to wear something that may not be decent. There are three motives I want to address concerning our choice of clothing: 1) ego building, 2) power and prestige, and 3) approval or praise. These are closely linked. They all focus on self, but they are three distinct areas we need to consider.

Ego Building

Our egos can influence our clothing choices. We can either feel confident or deflated simply because of the clothing we're wearing. Recently, my husband and I hosted several couples for an evening. When one of the couples arrived, the wife looked especially beautiful. She had styled her hair and wore a beautiful outfit. Many of the women commented on how beautiful she looked. Later that week, she told me that it took all of her strength to be gracious and accept the compliments because she felt self-conscious about her shoes. She shared with me that she had also disregarded her husband's compliments, and how her response had created a tense situation between them. This all happened because she thought her shoes were ugly. By the time she told me the story, she thought it was funny, but when she was in the middle of the situation, she wasn't laughing.

I've felt embarrassed by clothing and shoes before. Our egos can be a powerful force to deal with, and can bring out our insecurities. Most of us are insecure to some extent. Even the most beautiful women can have deep insecurities about themselves and how they look. Insecurity about how we look can fill us with worry and anxiety, and make us completely miserable.

This can become fertile ground for Satan to tempt us with ungodly responses. If you are insecure, you may find that you compare yourself to other women. This can lead to sins such as jealousy and envy. Deep insecurity can lead us to being obsessed about the world's idea of beauty, and this obsession can be the root of many problems, such as eating disorders or other destructive behavior.

The irony of these responses to our insecurity is the impact it has on our inner beauty. While we obsess about our outward beauty, we are missing the greatest beauty of all. We must think spiritually to overcome this kind of insecurity. As Christian women, we have set our sights on a greater goal than just physical beauty – we want to be beautiful to God, too.

Power and Prestige

Clothing can give us a sense of power and prestige. How we dress can open doors. For a young girl, it may be that she has the admiration of her peers because she always has the latest styles. She may also have the attention of the boys around her. Regardless of our age, being able to turn a man's head gives us a feeling of power. "Girl power" is a modern day mantra, but women have known about this from the beginning. Why did Eve eat the forbidden fruit? Because Satan tempted her with being like God. The fact that Adam chose to eat it with her instead of obeying God shows Eve's power and influence in her relationship with Adam.

Another example that illustrates a woman's power and prestige is the story of Esther. Esther needed to get her husband, the king, to make a ruling that would save the Jewish people, but for thirty days he had not called for her. She had one option – to show up unannounced. It was a dangerous move. If he did not hold out the golden scepter, she would lose her life (Esther 4:11). We are told that she put on her royal robes. When the king saw her standing there, he reached out his golden scepter and she walked up and touched it. He was so smitten by Esther that he offered her anything she wanted, up to half of his vast kingdom. This was a red carpet entrance that made history!

Esther's past experience had taught her how to make herself beautiful for the king. An edict had been issued to bring beautiful virgins to the king's harem so he could choose his next queen. Esther most likely did not want to be in this contest, but in her culture, if an order was sent to a family directing that their daughter go to the palace, the parents, however unwilling, dared not refuse the honor for their daughter. Although they knew that they would never see her again once she was in the royal harem, they were obliged to yield a silent and passive compliance.[26]

After Esther arrived at the harem, she went through a year of beauty treatments. When it was her turn to meet the king for the first time, she could have picked anything she wanted from the closets of the harem. She wisely asked for advice on what to wear, and she won the favor of the king. In fact, she won the favor of everyone who saw her.

Esther's experience had taught her how to turn her husband's head, but she also made herself spiritually beautiful. She had fasted and prayed for three days, seeking God's help in this challenging time.

She wasn't relying only on her physical beauty and beautiful clothing, she was also spiritually clothed with strength.

> She is clothed with strength and dignity; she can laugh at the days to come.
>
> Proverbs 31:25

Girl power is real and opens doors of opportunity. However, using physical beauty in this way can be costly. We have all seen beautiful, talented women lose their dignity while using their beauty to get something they wanted. They may have some short-term success, but in the long run, their lives are more a picture of weakness than of power. Outward beauty without inner beauty is, at best, a fleeting success. Lasting power and prestige come from our spiritual adornment, and it will never fade.

Approval and Praise

Do you dress to gain approval? Are you an approval and praise *junkie*? Does how you feel about yourself depend on whether or not someone gives you a compliment? This is one of the ways our insecurities can attack us.

Approval or praise can actually feel pretty good. I've noticed on many occasions how approval flows through women's conversations in the form of compliments. And a nice compliment about how you look can lift your spirit. Last year, I spent a weekend with three of my girlfriends. I had just begun my study of spiritual beauty and purity. It was eye-opening to see how often we complimented each other during the weekend. Our conversations were salted with compliments about each other's clothing, shoes, purses, hairstyles, jewelry, and so forth.

Expressing approval about each other's choices is a very natural response, but we need to be careful that approval and praise is not our goal. Trying to find security in our lives through the approval and praise of others can leave us feeling empty. It can also lead us to do things that are ungodly, including wearing things that are not decent. *Sophrosyne* (a constant rein on our passions and desires) is a great beauty secret of the soul that will help us overcome these insecurities. It will help us develop confidence in who we are. It will help us adopt a standard of purity that we can hold on to in our lives.

When I find that I'm insecure, I ask myself, "Who am I trying to please?" This helps me overcome my insecurities and focus on what is really the most important. We need to make sure that we seek God's approval first, and do not conform to worldly standards:

> *Charm is deceptive, and beauty is fleeting; but a woman who fears the LORD is to be praised. Give her the reward she has earned, and let her works bring her praise at the city gate.*
> Proverbs 31:30-31

* * *

We can feel a lot of pressure as a result of how we feel about our appearance. Digging out the *why* behind our clothing choices and looking our insecurities squarely in the face will help us overcome these pressures. It's a necessary step toward developing our inner beauty. No matter what our age, our motives are important to consider. Beauty that is driven by insecurities can leave us feeling empty. But spiritual beauty is lasting, unfading and fulfilling.

Worksheet 6 - Motives of the Heart

1. Do you look to fashion as a way to overcome insecurities? If so, how will having the right motives help you?

2. What motivates your choice of clothing?

Memory Verse: Psalms 51:10

– Chapter 7 –

Pure Entertainment

Entertainment can be music, a novel, a nail-biting drama, or competitive sports – anything that pleases or amuses us. It can be something we enjoy as a participant (or a virtual participant through computers) or just as a fan. This is another area of our lives that we need to purify:

> *Therefore, since Christ suffered in his body, arm yourselves also with the same attitude, because he who has suffered in his body is done with sin. As a result, he does not live the rest of his earthly life for evil human desires, but rather for the will of God. For you have spent enough time in the past doing what pagans choose to do--living in debauchery, lust, drunkenness, orgies, carousing and detestable idolatry.*
>
> 1 Peter 4:1-3

Our relationship with Jesus must be the foundation for everything we choose, including our entertainment. How you choose to be entertained says a lot about your heart.

Just like the moving standard of decency in clothing, the standard of what is morally acceptable in movies, television, music, books, video games, and so forth, seems to continually erode. In the 1930s, the movie industry adopted standards in an effort to provide wholesome entertainment. The following is an excerpt from the Motion Picture Production Code written at that time:

No picture shall be produced that will lower the moral standards of those who see it. Hence the sympathy of the audience should never be thrown to the side of crime, wrongdoing, evil or sin.

These shall never be presented in such a way as to throw sympathy with the crime as against law and justice or to inspire others with a desire for imitation.

The sanctity of the institution of marriage and the home shall be upheld. Pictures shall not infer that low forms of sexual relationships are the accepted or common thing.

Indecent or undue exposure is forbidden.[27]

Obviously, these standards no longer guide the motion picture industry. It's a rare movie that does not have a scene or a theme of immoral sex somewhere in the plot. Even movies about grand themes, often romanticize an immoral relationship. And without godly standards in movies and television, we can find ourselves pulled into the fray, laughing at impurity and rooting for someone to get together in an immoral relationship.

We need to consider carefully what we call entertainment and what God might think about our choices. For example, what about movies and television shows that promote homosexuality, adultery or sex before marriage? Can you imagine Jesus laughing at the punch lines? I can't because Genesis 6:5 says that man's wickedness grieves God. How can we laugh at something that grieves him? How can we call it entertainment? Our criteria needs to be broader than the question, "Will I struggle with impurity if I watch this." We need to also consider whether God would want us to watch it.

I enjoy watching movies about heros, romance, drama and comedy. I love to watch an underdog be victorious. However, I watch fewer and fewer of today's television shows and movies because of the immoral content and themes.

The Apostle Paul acknowledges in 1 Corinthians 5:9-10 that to completely disassociate yourself from immoral people, you have to leave this world. Practically speaking, we can't do that, but we can make godly choices about entertainment. Consider what Paul says about ungodliness, and how to think about it in our own lives:

> *For you were once darkness, but now you are light in the Lord. Live as children of light (for the fruit of the light consists in all goodness, righteousness and truth) and find out what pleases the Lord. Have nothing to do with the fruitless deeds of darkness, but rather expose them. For it is shameful even to mention what the disobedient do in secret.*
>
> Ephesians 5:8-12

This is certainly a good guideline to follow when we are choosing our entertainment. Considering what pleases the Lord will help us turn the channel more often.

* * *

Another way entertainment standards have slipped is evident in the latest wave of forensic science, crime-solving shows. Many of these new shows feature gruesome shots of women being brutalized and terrorized in very graphic, extended ways. The following is an excerpt from an article entitled, "TV Terror":

> The look of sheer terror in the woman's eyes is enough to make even the strongest stomach clench. When she realizes she has been kidnapped and can't get out of her captor's car, her eyes futilely dart to the left and to the right. She shouts and whack – a hard slap comes slamming across her face. The end seems near. Yet the writers of the new CBS drama "Criminal Minds" take the slow torture of an attractive, young female victim as something to be drawn out ever so slowly.
>
> Jeffrey Sconce, an associate professor of radio, television and film at Northwestern University, says, "Sadistic is the only word to use for some of these shows . . ."[28]

If you compare these television shows today with those watched five or ten years ago, you can see how much the standards regarding violence have declined. The following verses explain that we can actually crave more and more violence:

From the fruit of his lips a man enjoys good things, but the unfaithful have a craving for violence.

Proverbs 13:2

Having lost all sensitivity, they have given themselves over to sensuality so as to indulge in every kind of impurity, with a continual lust for more.

Ephesians 4:19

We can see why standards erode. The more we sin, the less sensitivity we have to what is evil. The result is a "continual lust for more." That is why we see more and more violence in movies and televisions shows today. When we are considering watching something that is violent, we need to consider the long-term impact it can have on our hearts and how God feels about it:

The LORD examines the righteous, but the wicked and those who love violence his soul hates.

Psalms 11:5

* * *

Another ungodly form of "entertainment" is pornography. You may think you would never watch porn, but over the last few decades, pornographic images have become more and more acceptable in A-list movies. Pornography is anything that is viewed for sexual arousal. And many movies have included scenes just for that purpose. Sex sells, and movies are made with that in mind.

Pornography is a $57 billion industry worldwide, and revenue from pornography is larger than the revenues of all professional football, baseball and basketball franchises combined.[29] Pornography is more than conveniently available – television and the internet make it difficult to keep out of your home.

Pornography is dangerous and destructive, and it has destroyed many marriages and families. It is like a drug that demands you take more and more. Today, many people face addictions to pornography, and this addiction has serious consequences in their lives. One danger is that it can destroy the intimacy of a marriage (or a future marriage). If you are married and you watch sexy or pornographic movies to "get in the mood," you are damaging your intimacy as a couple. (We will look at this in greater detail in the next chapter.)

The Internet

The internet, although a great resource, has little or no meaningful censorship. It is estimated that there are over 4.2 million pornographic websites that generate $2.5 billion a year in revenues.[30]

The internet is a source of many temptations. One temptation that can seem harmless is its social appeal. Chat rooms can have quite a pull for a woman who is lonely, but cyber relationships with strangers can actually lead to more loneliness by causing her to neglect real life relationships. Chat rooms are a poor way to build a relationship because you get a distorted view of the person with whom you are chatting. There is no accountability for what is said, and you have no idea about the person's reputation. It is a dangerous way to attempt to make social connections. Another problem is that you can get emotionally involved before you really know the person. Movies have glamorized the internet connection, but that is not the real world of the internet. A healthy relationship has to be built in person.

* * *

The internet offers many forms of entertainment. Our cyber entertainment is another opportunity for us to honor God by our choices.

> *I will set before my eyes no vile thing. The deeds of faithless men I hate; they will not cling to me. Men of perverse heart shall be far from me; I will have nothing to do with evil.*
>
> Psalms 101:3-4

* * *

Note to Parents:

If you have children, be sure you monitor their computer use. I've known parents who had stricter rules about telephone use than their children's use of computers. If you don't understand the internet and your child uses it regularly, you need to become aware of the dangers associated with web communities such as *Facebook* and *My Space,* and the risks children face who use them. Would you allow your child to talk with a total stranger for a long period of time on the telephone? I doubt it! You need to know who they are chatting with on the internet too. The internet offers our children some wonderful resources, including wholesome forms of entertainment. Make sure you know the hazards they may encounter on the internet, and help them make good choices.

Worksheet 7 - Pure Entertainment

1. What are your guidelines for entertainment?

2. Have you seen your own standards slip in any way concerning your choice of music, movies or television?

3. What scriptures have helped you most when it comes to choosing your entertainment?

Memory Verse: Psalms 101:3-4

– Chapter 8 –

Sexual Purity

But among you there must not be even a hint of sexual immoral-
ity, or of any kind of impurity, or of greed, because these are
improper for God's holy people.

Ephesians 5:3

Many people are misinformed about what constitutes sexual immorality and impurity. Even some who claim to be Christians say that
as long as you love each other, premarital sex is not a sin. Others have
a very narrow definition of adultery, and believe that technically they
have not committed adultery even though they have had a sexual encounter with someone who is not their spouse. Let's consider how
Jesus defined adultery:

You have heard that it was said, "Do not commit adultery."
But I tell you that anyone who looks at a woman lustfully has
already committed adultery with her in his heart.

Matthew 5:27-28

Jesus defined adultery more broadly than just the physical act. You
can be guilty of adultery even though you have not physically committed the act. He explains why in the following verse:

For out of the heart come evil thoughts, murder, adultery, sexu-
al immorality, theft, false testimony, slander.

Matthew 15:19

Jesus gives us valuable insight into our hearts – sin begins in your heart. Purifying our hearts is just as important as purifying our actions. 1 Corinthians 7:1 tells us to purify both body and spirit, in other words, not only our outward actions, but also our thoughts (mind) and emotional longings (heart).

I find this to be both good and bad news. Bad news because I'm guilty of a lot more sin than I initially thought I was; and good news because I now know how to fight this battle for purity. To illustrate, if we want to purify polluted air, water or land, the best place to start is the source of the pollution. The source of sexual impurity is the heart, so that's where we need to begin. However, our hearts present a unique and difficult challenge:

> *The heart is deceitful above all things and beyond cure. Who can understand it?*
>
> Jeremiah 17:9

We can be deceived by our own hearts. This means we accept something for truth that is a lie. But this does not mean we are without hope, because this is another area where turning to God's word will help us.

> *For the word of God is living and active. Sharper than any double-edged sword, it penetrates even to dividing soul and spirit, joints and marrow; <u>it judges the thoughts and attitudes of the heart</u>.* [Emphasis added.]
>
> Hebrews 4:12

Without God, we could not understand our hearts, but with the help of his word, we can judge what is in our hearts and begin to purify them. Let's consider some of the deceptions we face regarding sexual impurity, and what the Bible has to say about these deceptions. The following are a few common deceptions:

- I can handle this temptation.

- It doesn't hurt anyone.

- It's my business what I do.

- It's not really that bad.

- Sex before marriage is okay as long as you love each other.

These deceptions are dangerous because, if we believe them, we will face consequences both now and later. These consequences are eternal, as well as being physical and emotional.

Eternal Consequences

Put to death, therefore, whatever belongs to your earthly nature: sexual immorality, impurity, lust, evil desires and greed, which is idolatry. Because of these, the wrath of God is coming.

Colossians 3:5-6

Therefore, get rid of all moral filth and the evil that is so prevalent and humbly accept the word planted in you, which can save you.

James 1:21

The Bible contains many warnings and promises about our eternal destiny. The following scriptures list sexual sins that can have eternal consequences:

The acts of the sinful nature are obvious: sexual immorality [moicheia] [porneia], impurity [akatharsia] and debauchery [aselgeia] . . . I warn you, as I did before, that those who live like this will not inherit the kingdom of God.

Galatians 5:19-21

Do you not know that the wicked will not inherit the kingdom of God? Do not be deceived: Neither the sexually immoral [pornos] nor idolaters nor adulterers [moichos] nor male prostitutes nor homosexual offenders [arsenokoitēs] nor thieves nor the greedy nor drunkards nor slanderers nor swindlers will inherit the kingdom of God.

1 Corinthians 6:9-10

To better understand these scriptures, consider the meanings of the Greek words shown above in brackets:

- Adultery (*moicheia* and *moichos*) specifically means voluntary sexual intercourse between a man and woman who are not married to each other, where one or both are married to another person.

- Sexual immorality (*porneia* and *pornos*) is broader than *moicheia* and *moichos*. It includes adultery, incest and any voluntary sexual intercourse between a man and a woman who are not married to each other.

- Impurity (*akatharsia*) means physical or moral uncleanness. This would include voluntary behavior with another person outside of marriage that is sexual in nature.

- Debauchery (*aselgeia*) means that which is an insolent (boldly disrespectful) disregard of decency and an absence of restraint.

- Homosexual offenders (*arsenokoitēs*) means men having sex with men and women having sex with women.[31]

The Bible states that sexual immorality and impurity are obvious sins that will keep us out of heaven. But eternal consequences can seem unreal and difficult to grasp. First, they are experienced after death. It is only by faith that we act upon this warning. Second, we have been greatly influenced by worldly thinking. The world asks, "How can a loving God send someone to hell?" So they reason God will not judge them and they deliberately keep on sinning.

It is true that God is loving. In fact, he so loved us that he willingly sacrificed his only son in order for us to come into a relationship with him (John 3:16). But to think we do not need to obey God is a dangerous deception.

> *If we deliberately keep on sinning after we have received the knowledge of the truth, no sacrifice for sins is left, but only a fearful expectation of judgment and of raging fire that will consume the enemies of God.*
>
> Hebrews 10:26-27

True Christians cannot have even a hint of sexual immorality or impurity in their lives (Ephesians 5:3). This is a hard-line teaching, but obeying it protects us not only from eternal consequences, but also from physical and emotional consequences.

* * *

Physical Consequences

One of the deceptions regarding sexual impurity is that it doesn't hurt anybody. Consider these biblical warnings:

> *Flee from sexual immorality. All other sins a man commits are outside his body, but he who sins sexually sins against his own body.*
>
> 1 Corinthians 6:18

> *Therefore God gave them over in the sinful desires of their hearts to sexual impurity for the degrading of their bodies with one another.*
>
> Romans 1:24

Sexual immorality is actually a sin against your own body. This is evident from the damage caused by sexually transmitted diseases. STDs can cause infections of the reproductive organs, including infertility, ectopic pregnancy, abscess formation, chronic pelvic pain, cancer and even death. The consequences of STDs can be devastating and long-term. Although substantial progress has been made in the prevention, diagnoses, and treatment of certain STDs, an estimated 19 million new infections occur every year in the U.S.

Human papillomavirus, or HPV, is the name of a group of viruses that includes more than 100 different strains. More than 30 of these viruses are sexually transmitted. About 20 million people are currently infected with HPV, and every year in the U.S., about 6.2 million people get HPV. It is the major cause of cervical cancer.[32]

The most deadly STD is HIV/AIDS. Globally, over 25 million people have died of AIDS since 1981, and an estimated 33 to 46 million people are living with HIV/AIDS.[33] The serious physical consequences of sexual impurity show us that God did not create our bodies for multiple sex partners.

Besides STDs, another possible physical consequence of sexual impurity is an unwanted pregnancy. This can change the course of a woman's life. She may feel forced into marriage, or she may choose to raise her child by herself and face the challenges of being a single mom. She may give up her child for adoption and deal with emotional challenges for years. Or she may add another sin to her life (along with a lot of emotional pain) by ending her unborn child's life by abortion. Since abortion was legalized in 1973, over 47 million women in the United States have had an abortion.[34]

When we understand the consequences of sexual impurity, we can see more clearly the wisdom God offers us in the Bible. God's principles regarding sexual purity are not burdensome rules – instead, they are for our own protection.

> *"For the waywardness of the simple will kill them, and the complacency of fools will destroy them; but whoever listens to me will live in safety and be at ease, without fear of harm."*
>
> Proverbs 1:32-33

God created Adam and Eve to live in a monogamous relationship (Genesis 2:24). Here is what Jesus said about the relationship God designed for them:

> *"Haven't you read," he replied, "that at the beginning the Creator 'made them male and female,' and said, 'For this reason a man will leave his father and mother and be united to his wife, and the two will become one flesh'? So they are no longer two, but one. Therefore what God has joined together, let man not separate."*
>
> Matthew 19:4-6

Even the Centers for Disease Control and Prevention advises living in a long-term, mutually monogamous relationship to prevent STDs. Thinking that safe sexual practices will prevent all STDs is false security. The CDC says an HPV infection can occur in both male and female genital areas even if they are covered or protected by a latex condom, as well as in areas that are not covered. It is estimated that at least 50 percent of sexually active men and women will acquire a genital HPV infection at some point in their lives.[35]

Sexual impurity can bring with it many physical challenges and hardships. When someone says that sexual impurity is okay because nobody gets hurt, they are deceived.

* * *

Emotional Consequences

One of the many emotional consequences of sexual impurity is that we do not get to enjoy the fruit of the Holy Spirit. As you read the following passage, contrast the emotional consequences of the sins listed below with the emotions we enjoy through the qualities of the Holy Spirit.

> *The acts of the sinful nature are obvious: sexual immorality, impurity and debauchery; idolatry and witchcraft; hatred, discord, jealousy, fits of rage, selfish ambition, dissensions, factions and envy; drunkenness, orgies, and the like. I warn you, as I did before, that those who live like this will not inherit the kingdom of God. But the fruit of the Spirit is love, joy, peace, patience, kindness, goodness, faithfulness, gentleness and self-control. Against such things there is no law. Those who belong to Christ Jesus have crucified the sinful nature with its passions and desires. Since we live by the Spirit, let us keep in step with the Spirit. [Emphasis added.]*
>
> Galatians 5:22-24

Sin has enormous emotional consequences; for example, the negative emotional experience of contracting an STD or of an unwanted pregnancy. The above verse shows us that we cannot have emotional well being – the fruit of the Spirit – while living a life of sin. This is true of any of the sins listed above. It may take more time for some of the consequences to show themselves, but they will eventually.

To overcome sexual impurity, it helps to understand our sexual and emotional longings and how these desires can lead to impurity and serious consequences. While most men are tempted visually, women are more apt to be tempted through their emotions. Movies we call "chick flicks" show the knight in shining armor or prince charming rescuing the damsel in distress. My personal favorite is the story of Cinderella. In the end of the story, Cinderella marries her prince. Movie after movie is based on this and similar themes because it appeals to our emotions.

Book sales also indicate how much women are drawn by their emotional longings to the knight-in-shining-armor kind of guy. Romance books generated $1.2 billion in sales in 2004, and 78% of the 64.6 million Americans who read at least one romance novel were women.[36]

I am not saying that a Christian should not watch romantic movies or read a romantic book, but we need to understand why we are attracted to these things and the impact they can have on our lives. A married woman, for example, may be tempted to turn to these things as a substitute for an emotional connection with her husband. A common deception is that fantasies are no big deal and that no one gets hurt. If you are married, fantasizing about someone else will damage your intimacy as a couple. You cannot be one with your husband and be intimately connected when you are imagining that you are with another man.

If you tend to get emotionally connected with male characters you see in movies, you must remember that their lives are just pretend. This is not real life, and you should not compare your husband to what you see on the screen. First, it's not fair. In real life, most of these actors cannot even stay married, or they are bachelors who go from one relationship to another. They may be handsome and romantic men, but they are only following a script and acting the part in front of a camera. And they get as many retakes as necessary. Second, you can do a lot of damage to your relationship by comparing your husband to these produced and directed superhero kind of guys. Who can live up to that kind of fantasy? I know women married to wonderful Christian men who do not appreciate their husbands because they're always comparing them to the man in their fantasy.

We must guard our hearts. Affairs of the heart can do a lot of damage to the intimacy of your marriage. Oneness in marriage involves our emotions and thoughts as well as our physical relationship. This means we must be pure emotionally, mentally and physically. If you are married, it means your husband is the only one you have sexual thoughts about, and he is the only one with whom you have sex. Emotional and mental purity means that you guard your feelings and thoughts concerning other men, and you do not fantasize about being with another man. Emotional, mental and physical purity are foundations for greater intimacy.

Consider the difference in the levels of intimacy in the following examples. Which would you rather have in your marriage?

1) When you spend time together sexually, you are thinking of another man (fictional or real) and your husband is thinking of another woman;

or

2) When you spend time together sexually, you shut out the world, enjoy an intimate bond, and are devoted to each other emotionally, mentally and physically?

Of course, this choice is like the old deli meat commercial that asked, "Do you want this delicious sandwich made with our deli meat or do you want the sandwich run over by a bus?" Certainly, I want a great marriage with the purest intimacy with my husband. I want to desire only him and want his desire to be only for me. And I want this close bond throughout my marriage.

God doesn't want the run-over-by-a-bus life for us either. He designed us to be one in marriage with complete unity. He created sex to be a fulfilling part of marriage, and he gives us the inside scoop on how to have an intimate relationship. His commands about sexual purity are for our protection and benefit.

Impurity in marriage has a big price tag. Watching sexually stimulating movies with pornographic images will break down emotional intimacy. If you are aroused emotionally and sexually by a movie, instead of by your husband, you are looking to someone else to fulfill you. Things that tear down a couple's emotional intimacy can begin a downward spiral that leads to much more sin and much less sexual fulfillment. Married couples who get involved in orgies and spouse swapping are an extreme case. No couple starts off their marriage thinking they will ever get involved in such gross sexual sins. But increasing impurity can lead to such sinful behavior.

What about the typical challenges that Christian couples face that are not so extreme? One common temptation regarding sexual purity is addressed in this passage:

> *The husband should fulfill his marital duty to his wife, and like-wise the wife to her husband. The wife's body does not belong to her alone but also to her husband. In the same way, the husband's body does not belong to him alone but also to his wife. Do not deprive each other except by mutual consent and for a time, so that you may devote yourselves to prayer. Then come together again <u>so that Satan will not tempt you</u> because of your lack of self-control.* [Emphasis added.]
>
> 1 Corinthians 7:3-5

This passage gives a very important guideline to married couples: do not withhold yourselves sexually from each other, except for an agreed-upon limited time for the purpose of prayer. If you withhold yourself sexually from your husband, you need to understand how Satan will use this against you and your husband. There are several things that can happen. It can erode any intimacy you have already built. It can also create fertile ground for more impurity in both of you, and begin a downward spiral in your relationship. If you are feeling emotionally disconnected, the answer isn't less sex. That will only lead to more challenges.

(When I say "emotionally disconnected," I am referring to the day-to-day issues in life that can create a distance between a wife and husband, such as finances, parenting, busy schedules, disagreements, and so forth. I am not talking about a woman who has an unfaithful husband or couples who face critical and complicated issues that require special counseling.)

We need to understand that it is Satan who tempts us to withhold ourselves sexually from our spouses. He aims to destroy your marriage. This is one of the most critical spiritual battles a married couple will face, because it can cause so many other problems in the marriage relationship.

If you are married and don't find your sexual relationship exciting, how do you turn it around? First, you must root out impurity on every level – physically, emotionally and mentally. You may find this challenging, especially in terms of emotional and mental purity, if you have freely fantasized about being with other men. It will most likely take determination to overcome this pattern in your life. But it will be worth the effort because growing in your purity will create a foundation for greater intimacy with your husband.

The idea of growing in your purity is the opposite of what the world says will build a better sexual relationship in marriage. The world says that forbidden things are the way to improve your sexual relationship. I recently picked up a magazine that had an article about ten fantasies to think about to help you get in the mood for sex. The majority were indecent things that a true Christian would not even think about doing. Embracing more of the world and turning to ungodly things is not the answer to a dull sex life with your spouse. You may be stimulated by a sexy or pornographic movie, or by fantasizing about being with another man, but over time it will take a toll on your intimacy as a couple. Many couples, both Christian and non-Christian, can have an exciting sexual relationship for a short time, but marriage is "till death do us part." This is not a time to be shortsighted or faithless about God's call for us to be sexually pure in body and spirit.

There are many ways to enhance your sexual relationship that do not involve impurity. Evaluate how you spend your time. If you lead a crazy time-crunched life, you will very likely be too tired for the things that build intimacy with your spouse. And if you don't take the time necessary to build your togetherness, you will have less sexual desire for each other. This is a pit many couples fall into. But a greater pitfall can happen when trying to remedy this problem by listening to ungodly advice. The world says do forbidden things to get in the mood for sex, but the real solution is to look at what you do to build intimacy – an intimacy where you can shut out the world and enjoy an intimate bond with each other, one where you are connected emotionally, mentally and physically. God's solution is always better!

Sometimes a couple needs more information about the physiological aspects of sex to know what heightens sexual pleasure. There are books such as *Intended for Pleasure* by Ed Wheat that explain these things. God created sex to be a wonderful long-term blessing of marriage that bonds us into an amazing intimacy that he describes as becoming one. This special bond in marriage can only be built through purity.

* * *

For a single woman, sexual purity means that she is pure physically, emotionally and mentally. Being single does not mean she is free to have ungodly fantasies about a man who catches her eye. She can dream about having a husband some day, but her dreams must be righteous. Earlier we looked at the Greek word *sophrosyne,* which means a constant rein on all passions and desires. This is a quality that will help keep those dreams pure before God. (More about this later.)

There may be much more at stake than you realize. If you are single and hope to marry some day, but have affairs of the heart, you may never find a man who lives up to your fantasy. Or if you marry, you may find your prince is less exciting than the one in your fantasies. This may lead to challenges in your new marriage.

Being pure physically, mentally and emotionally when you are single will give you an opportunity to build greater intimacy if you marry someday. Or if you continue your life as a single, purity will give you peace. Peace, a quality of the Holy Spirit, is one of the blessings of purity that we can enjoy whether we are married or single.

> *The mind of sinful man is death, but the mind controlled by the Spirit is <u>life and peace</u> . . .* [Emphasis added.]
>
> Romans 8:6

> *So then, dear friends, since you are looking forward to this, make every effort to be <u>found spotless, blameless and at peace with him</u>.* [Emphasis added.]
>
> 2 Peter 3:14

* * *

How pure do we need to be and how much effort should I put into this? Ephesians 5:3 says that there must not be even a hint of sexual immorality or any kind of impurity. This can seem like an unrealistic expectation if you do not understand the dangers of impurity.

You were taught, with regard to your former way of life, to put off your old self, <u>which is being corrupted</u> [phtheirō] by its deceitful desires; to be made new in the attitude of your minds; and to put on the new self, created to be like God in true righteousness and holiness. [Emphasis added.]

Ephesians 4:22-24

The Greek word translated "corrupted" is *phtheirō.*

Definition: *Phtheirō* (fthi'-ro); to spoil (by any process) to ruin (especially figurative by moral influences, to deprave); corrupt (self), defile, destroy.[37]

Impurity corrupts our lives, but we may be tempted to ignore the danger because the consequences are not immediate. Just like when Eve ate the forbidden fruit, she did not immediately die. We can also ignore the warning because we think that the consequences are not that bad. The seriousness of the consequences are sometime hidden from us. However, this does not mean the danger is not real. There are many hidden dangers in our world that we know about and act upon, such as the dangers of lead poisoning. Lead poisoning can reduce a child's IQ, slow his growth, cause hearing problems and damage kidneys.[38] The symptoms are not immediately seen, but we know there is a real danger. We do not want to allow even a hint of lead poisoning in our homes. The same must be true concerning impurity. It is a very real danger.

Not all of the consequences of impurity are hidden. For example, we can see the fallacies of the world's wisdom concerning sexual fulfillment. At first, the world's wisdom looks promising, but in the end, it leads to heartache and emptiness. The proof of their heartaches surrounds us. When my children were preteens and teens, I bought *People* magazines with photos splashed across the cover of famous couples, who said they were madly in love. I would put the magazine away until the breakup was announced, then I would buy that issue as well. (I seldom had to wait very long.) Then I would show both articles to my children, and talk about the wisdom of God's way versus the world's way. I would ask them what they thought happened to a couple who earlier claimed to be so in love, but were now saying they hate each

81

other. We would discuss how the world says to make your own rules and do whatever feels good, but how God teaches us to be pure in our dating and marriage relationships. God's way is one in which we build a great friendship and wait until marriage for a sexual relationship, and then enjoy a lifetime together.

These magazine articles gave a profound picture of the cost of ignoring the wisdom of God. And this pattern with Hollywood's couples was repeated over and over again. These vivid pictures still line the checkout counters at grocery stores. My intent is not to indict every couple in Hollywood. But for the most part, the wisdom we read in the popular magazines is not true wisdom, and the proof is right in front of our eyes. God offers incredible wisdom on how to have a fulfilling sexual relationship. The more we purify ourselves sexually, the greater opportunity we have for an intimate and lifelong bond with our spouse (or future spouse).

* * *

As we strive for purity, we must believe that it is possible. We hear too often from "experts" who say that we can't change. The following scripture shows that we can.

> *Do you not know that the wicked will not inherit the kingdom of God? Do not be deceived: Neither the sexually immoral nor idolaters nor adulterers nor male prostitutes nor homosexual offenders nor thieves nor the greedy nor drunkards nor slanderers nor swindlers will inherit the kingdom of God. <u>And that is what some of you were</u>. But you were washed, you were sanctified, you were justified in the name of the Lord Jesus Christ and by the Spirit of our God.* [Emphasis added.]
> 1 Corinthians 6:9-11

No matter what our background, by faith we can purge the impurities out of our lives. And the more we do so, the more godliness and intimacy we will enjoy.

> *Since we have these promises, dear friends, let us purify [katharizo] ourselves from everything that contaminates body and spirit, perfecting holiness out of reverence for God.*
> 2 Corinthians 7:1

Definition: *Katharizō* (kath-ar-id´-zo); to cleanse (literal or figurative); make clean, purge, purify.[39]

The definition uses the word "purge" to explain the Greek word *katharizo*. Purging something out of our lives will take effort. We may have to break old habits or work through deep-seated issues. The good news is that we *can* purify ourselves. In the following chapters, we will look at how God equips us to purify our thoughts and our hearts.

Worksheet 8 - Sexual Purity

1. What are some common deceptions we face today with regard to sexual impurity?

2. What scriptures can help us see the truth about these deceptions?

3. Do you allow yourself to have affairs of the heart? If so, what impact does this have on your purity?

Memory Verse: Ephesians 5:3

– Chapter 9 –

Pure Thoughts

The LORD detests the thoughts of the wicked, but those of the pure are pleasing to him.

Proverbs 15:26

God is not only concerned with our actions; his feelings are stirred by what we think! According to Genesis 6:5, God was grieved and his heart filled with pain because the thoughts of men were evil. Our thoughts, good and bad, move God.

We also see Jesus' feelings about impure thoughts and attitudes in his sharp statement to the Pharisees:

"Woe to you, teachers of the law and Pharisees, you hypocrites! You clean the outside of the cup and dish, but inside they are full of greed and self-indulgence. Blind Pharisee! First clean the inside of the cup and dish, and then the outside also will be clean.

Matthew 23:25-26

It is the inside of the cup (our hearts and minds) that needs the most work. The truth is we can do a lot of good things, but still be full of impure thoughts and attitudes. This is unacceptable to God. The following proverb explains why our thoughts are so important:

For <u>as he thinks within himself, so he is</u>. He says to you, "Eat and drink!" But his heart is not with you. [Emphasis added.]

Proverbs 23:7 (NASB)

Your thoughts are the real you. I find this a little frightening because sometimes I do or say things because I know I should – not because my heart is in the right place. And if my thoughts were exposed, I would have some explaining to do! This confirms for me that I am in a real spiritual battle. And the biggest part of that battle will be won or lost in my mind. The Apostle Paul made this point when he described his spiritual battle as a war in his mind (Romans 7:21-25). He went on to explain how the Holy Spirit helps us win:

> Those who live according to the sinful nature have their <u>minds</u> set on what that nature desires; but those who live in accordance with the Spirit have their <u>minds</u> set on what the Spirit desires. The <u>mind</u> of sinful man is death, but the <u>mind</u> controlled by the Spirit is life and peace. [Emphasis added.]
>
> Romans 8:5-6

This passage describes two potential outcomes of our spiritual battle: <u>death</u> or <u>life and peace</u>. Notice how the mind is at the center of this battle. Purifying our minds is not just a nice idea, it is an absolute necessity.

Do you have a good picture of this battle? Compare one of your worst times to one of your best. Picture a day when your thoughts are centered on disappointment, worry or despair. Now compare that to a time when your thoughts are peaceful and faithful. Or compare a day when your mind is filled with sinful thoughts to a day when your thoughts are pure and guilt free. Other examples of this battle are hate versus love, frustration versus joy, and insecurity versus confidence.

Seeing this contrast of life and death helps me understand why God is as concerned with our thoughts and attitudes as he is with our actions and why so many scriptures teach us that we need to change our thinking. Here are a few examples:

> Do not conform any longer to the pattern of this world, but <u>be transformed by the renewing of your mind</u>. [Emphasis added.]
>
> Romans 12:2a

> You were taught, with regard to your former way of life, to put off your old self, which is being corrupted by its deceitful de-

86

sires; <u>to be made new in the attitude of your minds</u> . . .
[Emphasis added.]

Ephesians 4:22-23

Therefore, <u>prepare your minds for action</u>; be self-controlled; set your hope fully on the grace to be given you when Jesus Christ is revealed. [Emphasis added.]

1 Peter 1:13

* * *

In the last chapter, we looked at the harmful impact of sexually impure thoughts. We will now look at a broader range of impure thoughts – anger, rage, bitterness, greed, fear, insecurity, doubt, guilt, and the like. Any one of these can contaminate our spirits. If not dealt with, these thoughts have the potential to cause us to give up our faith in God, or at the very least, make us miserable.

What impure thoughts do you battle with the most? The following are some answers I've gotten to this question:

- I have thoughts that my husband doesn't love me.
- I have jealous thoughts about my husband's former relationship.
- I think about old boyfriends from before I became a Christian.
- I have sexual fantasies about someone other than my husband.
- I worry about whether my husband will be faithful to me.
- I worry, if my husband dies, what will happen to me and my children.
- I worry about money and my future.
- I have thoughts about bad things happening to me and my loved ones.
- I have thoughts about cutting, hurting or killing myself.
- I have thoughts of self-hatred.
- I have anxious thoughts about how I look (my clothes, my hair, my weight)

- I worry about what others think of me.

- I think God does not care about me.

Our spirits can be contaminated by a wide range of thoughts. Some thoughts may be a onetime occurrence, and others may be an obsession. Are you tuned in to the battle for a pure spirit? Do you know how to purify a hateful or selfish thought? The following scriptures show us where we can begin:

> *Those who live according to the sinful nature have their minds set [phroneo] on what that nature desires; but those who live in accordance with the Spirit have their minds set [phroneo] on what the Spirit desires.*
>
> Romans 8:5

> *Set your minds [phroneo] on things above, not on earthly things.*
>
> Colossians 3:2

The Greek word translated "minds set" or "set your mind" is *phroneo*.

Definition: *Phroneo* (fron-eh´-o); to exercise the mind; by implication to be mentally disposed, more or less earnestly, in a certain direction; an intensive interest in (with concern or obedience); set the affection on.[40]

By earnestly exercising our minds, we can change the way we think! We do not have to live with the unwanted thoughts listed above. What do you want to change in your thoughts? What negative "tapes" play in your mind during your most challenging moments?

There are three steps (or exercises) that I have found helpful to purify my thoughts: 1) recognize Satan's schemes; 2) take captive every impure thought; and 3) make every thought obedient to Christ.

1) Recognize Satan's Schemes

> *For <u>we are not unaware of his schemes</u>.* [Emphasis added.]
>
> 2 Corinthians 2:11b

> *Put on the full armor of God so that you can <u>take your stand against the devil's schemes</u>. For our struggle is not against flesh and blood, but against the rulers, against the authorities,*

against the powers of this dark world and against the spiritual forces of evil in the heavenly realms. [Emphasis added.]
Ephesians 6:11-12

We are at war with the spiritual forces of evil around us. It isn't a physical battle that you can see – it's a battle that takes place within us. And if we understand how Satan attacks us, we can fight him more effectively. His first avenue of attack is from inside our own hearts.

For out of the heart come evil thoughts . . .
Matthew 15:19

Destructive and evil thoughts can bubble up out of our hearts at any time. They include thoughts rooted in selfishness, pride or sensuality. For example, Satan may use a serious illness to tempt us to be bitter or faithless, or use past failures to tempt us to be insecure. He uses our sensual desires to tempt us to be impure, immoral or perverse.

Satan's second avenue of attack is from outside our hearts – the *"spiritual forces of evil in the heavenly realms."* This may sound like a science fiction movie, but this is the real deal. These forces are real and we face them every day. They press on us through the worldliness around us. It may be a song, an advertisement or a popular TV show. Our enemies, and even friends, can stir up an evil thought. Or perhaps it is a thought from out of the blue that's so strange or evil that you may wonder why you had such a thought. If you do not recognize Satan when he lays an evil thought at the door of your heart, you can easily lose the ensuing battle. And if you allow worldly thoughts to stay in your mind and dwell on them long enough, they will become your own.

Do you recognize the scheme Satan is using against you? It's tailor-made just for you. He has a plan to discourage and destroy you. Do you know how to fight back? Let's consider how Jesus fought Satan's schemes.

Then Jesus was led by the Spirit into the desert to be tempted by the devil. After fasting forty days and forty nights, he was hungry. The tempter came to him and said, "If you are the Son of God, tell these stones to become bread."

Jesus answered, "It is written: 'Man does not live on bread alone, but on every word that comes from the mouth of God.'"

89

Then the devil took him to the holy city and had him stand on the highest point of the temple. "If you are the Son of God," he said, "throw yourself down. For it is written: 'He will command his angels concerning you, and they will lift you up in their hands, so that you will not strike your foot against a stone.'"

Jesus answered him, "It is also written: 'Do not put the Lord your God to the test.'"

Again, the devil took him to a very high mountain and showed him all the kingdoms of the world and their splendor. "All this I will give you," he said, "if you will bow down and worship me."

Jesus said to him, "Away from me, Satan! For it is written: 'Worship the Lord your God, and serve him only.'"

Then the devil left him, and angels came and attended him.

Matthew 4:1-11

This scripture says, "The tempter came to him." It's not clear whether Satan came in an actual physical form or if this was a battle fought in Jesus' thoughts. Personally, I don't think Satan appeared to Jesus in a physical form, because the Bible says our struggle is not against flesh and blood. I picture Jesus in a very weakened state from going forty days without food. He saw a stone that looked like a loaf of bread and he thought, "*If you are the Son of God, tell these stones to become bread.*" Jesus immediately recognized that he was in a battle with Satan and answered him with scripture. Then Satan tempted Jesus to throw himself off the highest point of the temple. Jesus again answered him with scripture. Finally, with complete boldness, Satan did his best to get Jesus to bow down and worship him, but Jesus responded with scripture and told Satan to go away. Then the angels came and helped Jesus.

Physically, this would have been difficult to do. Could Jesus have walked up a very high mountain after fasting 40 days? In Luke's account of Jesus' temptation, he stated that the devil showed him all the kingdoms of the world in an instant. We don't know if Satan appeared to Jesus in a physical form, but we do know that Satan does not pop up to us that way. If he did appear to us – like the little devil often pictured in cartoons – our battle would be much easier to fight. "Hey, Satan, I'm not listening to you. Get out of my way!" Instead, Satan sneaks up on us in our thoughts.

We can experience the same kinds of temptations that Jesus did. We can doubt that we really are children of God. And when our faith is weak, we can be tempted to put God to the test. We can also be tempted to put things in the world ahead of God in order to make more money. These are common temptations. Do you recognize Satan when you are tempted? Satan can tempt us in the middle of the night when we are completely alone. He doesn't have to show up in a physical form to tempt us, yet we can still know for sure that he is the one we are battling!

In the following passage, Jesus recognized that Satan was using the words of His friend to tempt him:

> From that time on Jesus began to explain to his disciples that he must go to Jerusalem and suffer many things at the hands of the elders, chief priests and teachers of the law, and that he must be killed and on the third day be raised to life.
>
> Peter took him aside and began to rebuke him. "Never, Lord!" he said. "This shall never happen to you!"
>
> Jesus turned and said to Peter, "Get behind me, Satan! You are a stumbling block to me; you do not have in mind [phroneo] the things of God, but the things of men."
>
> Matthew 16:21-23

Satan made this temptation sound like good advice: "Jesus, you don't have to die." But again Jesus recognized Satan's scheme. Jesus told Peter that his thoughts were not from God. I doubt Peter had any idea that Satan was using him to tempt Jesus, but Jesus boldly called Satan out.

We must recognize Satan's schemes in the thoughts of our hearts and the forces of evil that surround us each day. Satan has a tailor-made scheme for each one of us. His schemes may not be obvious, and may even seem to be comforting. He can make a temptation look appealing and even righteous. When we learn to recognize his schemes as Jesus did, we will have much greater success in overcoming our temptations.

The following scripture explains how temptations lead to sin:

When tempted, no one should say, "God is tempting me." For God cannot be tempted by evil, nor does he tempt anyone; but each one is tempted when, by his own evil desire, he is dragged away and enticed. Then, after desire has conceived, it gives birth to sin; and sin, when it is full-grown, gives birth to death.
James 1:13-15

The battle begins when we are tempted. The temptation itself is not sin. We know that Jesus was tempted but he never sinned:

For we do not have a high priest who is unable to sympathize with our weaknesses, but we have one who has been tempted in every way, just as we are--yet was without sin. Let us then approach the throne of grace with confidence, so that we may receive mercy and find grace to help us in our time of need.
Hebrews 4:15-16

Jesus knows all about how we struggle to be pure, and he sympathizes with us. Isn't that comforting? But unlike Jesus, who never lost a battle with Satan, we have lost plenty. That's where *"our time of need"* comes in. The above verse says we can be confident when we go to God in our time of need. However, confidence is not our natural response when we are feeling needy. In *The Complete Guide to Grace* by my husband, James L. Lefler, he explains why we can be confident:

". . .God sees everything. That's scary because we think and do things we know are evil. Most of us try to maintain our image and control what we let the people around us see—we don't want them to know the real us. But we cannot hide anything from God. Think about your week. Did anything happen that you don't want to be held accountable for? Were you deceitful to avoid painful consequences? Did you have an ungodly attitude toward a co-worker or maybe another driver? God watched it all. God not only sees, he heard what you said in your heart. We are even accountable for our attitudes.

You may be asking, "So how will this help me be confident?" The fact that God knows us inside and out, but still loves us and wants a relationship with us helps give us confidence. He did not choose us because we were such good people. He knows every one of our shortcomings. In addition, Jesus is our "great high priest." He knows exactly how we feel and sympathizes with our weaknesses. He has been through similar battles Himself."[41]

Are you confident that God will help you? Too many of us believe God is great and powerful but struggle with whether He cares or even notices our lives. My husband's study of grace has radically changed my view of God. God is bigger, kinder and closer than I ever imagined. This has helped me hurry to God in my time of need. Understanding how much God wants to show us favor and how much he cares about the details in our lives is the greatest defense we can have against Satan's schemes. This will help us be much more effective at setting our minds on things above and recognizing when Satan's is trying to turn us away from God.

2) Take Every Thought Captive

We demolish arguments and every pretension that sets itself up against the knowledge of God, and we take captive every thought to make it obedient to Christ.

2 Corinthians 10:5

The second step that will help us change our thinking is to take every thought captive. In a war, if you take someone captive, you have control over their every move. You decide how much freedom your captives get. They can be locked up with no freedom at all, or you may allow them certain privileges.

The same is true of your thoughts. You have a choice – you can decide how much freedom you give a thought. You may decide it gets no freedom, or you may allow a thought to dwell in your mind even though you know you should not. You may give an impure thought freedom when you have been hurt or when you have spent time with someone who negatively influences your thinking, or perhaps when you are going through physical or financial challenges. It's important to realize that you have a choice.

I am not saying that taking a thought captive means we stuff it or ignore it. If we do that, we are more like the prisoner than the thought is. We must learn how to transform the thought.

93

When I first began to understand I could transform my thoughts, I was thrilled. This was a new concept to me. I could take a destructive, tempting, or negative thought and make it a "prisoner of war" – I could decide to give it no freedom. This was an exciting discovery for me; however, the excitement soon vanished when I realized that this was not an easy task. Learning how to take my thoughts captive was going to take determination and focus (exercise), especially the thoughts driven by my deepest insecurities. I needed to practice making these unwanted thoughts obedient to Christ.

3) Make Every Thought Obedient to Christ

The third step is where real progress is made. The first two steps – recognizing Satan's schemes and deciding you will give impure thoughts no freedom – are necessary steps, but the third step is where real change begins. When we obey the scriptures that give us direction about our thoughts, a transformation begins to take place, and God's divine power helps shape how we think. If you have been a Christian very long, you know what I'm talking about. Sometimes it is such a gradual process that you do not even notice it happening. Then one day, you realize how differently you think compared to a few years earlier.

Changing our thinking is a lifelong process. Satan will not give up in this spiritual battle as long as we live, so our best strategy is to fight aggressively for pure thoughts. We can do that by using some unusual weapons:

> For though we live in the world, we do not wage war as the world does. The weapons we fight with are not the weapons of the world. On the contrary, they have divine power to demolish strongholds.
>
> 2 Corinthians 10:3-4

With God's help, we can change thoughts driven by the deepest-seated issues (strongholds) in our lives. It may take some time, but we can completely change the way we think. Let's consider how to use some of these powerful weapons:

Prayer

> *Do not be anxious about anything, but in everything, by prayer and petition, with thanksgiving, <u>present your requests to God.</u> <u>And the peace of God,</u> which transcends all understanding, <u>will guard your hearts and your minds</u> in Christ Jesus.* [Emphasis added.]
>
> Philippians 4:6-7

Prayer is one of our most powerful weapons. Notice the promise in this verse. When we are anxious about something, we can present our request to God and his peace will guard our minds.

When I'm in the middle of a battle in my mind, whether it is driven by anger, worry, insecurity, bitterness, or greed, I consider what I need at that moment to help me. When I know what my request should be, I present it to God in prayer. I get specific about it, too. This is not the time for a general prayer. My prayer might be, "Father, help me turn my thoughts away from this bitterness, and remember how blessed I am to know you. Help me forgive deeply from my heart." Sometimes my thoughts are so overwhelming that I first have to ask God to help me clear my mind so that I can even begin to pray.

The promise in this passage is that he will guard your mind and give you peace beyond your understanding. I have experienced the peace promised in this verse. Sometimes it has taken some intense prayer, but I am amazed at how my anxiety can turn to peace following such a prayer. This is truly divine power.

Openness

> *If we claim to have fellowship with him yet walk in the darkness, we lie and do not live by the truth. But if we walk in the light, as he is in the light, we have fellowship with one another, and the blood of Jesus, his Son, purifies us from all sin.*
>
> *If we claim to be without sin, we deceive ourselves and the truth is not in us. If we confess our sins, he is faithful and just and will forgive us our sins and purify us from all unrighteousness.*
>
> 1 John 1:6-9

> *Therefore confess your sins to each other and pray for each*
> *other so that you may be healed. The prayer of a righteous man*
> *is powerful and effective.*
>
> James 5:16

Openness is an effective weapon that helps us change how we think, but many find it difficult to use. Even though we all struggle with similar things, it can be embarrassing to be open. The following scripture explains how common our temptations really are:

> *No temptation has seized you except what is common to man.*
> *And God is faithful; he will not let you be tempted beyond what*
> *you can bear. But when you are tempted, he will also provide a*
> *way out so that you can stand up under it.*
>
> 1 Corinthians 10:13

Satan wants you to think that you are the only one who struggles the way you do. He wants you to be alone in the dark. But the truth is our temptations are not unusual, and if we open up about them, we will be able to overcome them. James 5:16 says we can be healed.

I remember the first time I confessed some of my most embarrassing sins. I first asked God to make it clear who I could talk to about these things. It was difficult because I felt that a real Christian should not struggle with sin. But the truth is Christians do struggle:

> *If we claim to be without sin, we deceive ourselves and the truth*
> *is not in us.*
>
> 1 John 1:8

Do you have a discipleship partner or a close spiritual friend to whom you can confess your sins and temptations? If not, develop a closer relationship with a Christian sister, who can give you helpful insight that you may not be able to achieve on your own. Openness is an effective way to fight Satan.

The above scriptures about confession deal with sin rather than temptation, but I encourage you to also be open about your temptations. You will take away much of Satan's power in your thoughts when you are open about your temptations. Satan cannot stand in the light. The following scripture explains obstacles we must overcome to be open:

> *This is the verdict: Light has come into the world, but men loved darkness instead of light because their deeds were evil. Everyone who does evil hates the light, and will not come into the light for fear that his deeds will be exposed. But whoever lives by the truth comes into the light, so that it may be seen plainly that what he has done has been done through God.*
>
> John 3:19-21

The thought of being open about sin can stir up our fears, but openness is another weapon with divine power. Keep it close to you. You will have to fight to stay open because Satan hates the light. He hates it because it will give you strength and bring God glory for what is happening in your life (John 3:21).

Meditation

> *May the words of my mouth and the meditation of my heart be pleasing in your sight, O LORD, my Rock and my Redeemer.*
>
> Psalms 19:14

> *I have hidden your word in my heart that I might not sin against you.*
>
> Psalms 119:11

Meditation is another useful weapon that helps us change how we think. (To meditate means to reflect upon, study or ponder.[42]) Just like Jesus, we too need to keep God's word close to our hearts to help us in our battles with Satan. We can do this through daily Bible study, memorizing key scriptures and taking time to ponder what we are learning as we go about our day. The following verses describe the Bible as a sword:

> *Take the helmet of salvation and the sword of the Spirit, which is the word of God.*
>
> Ephesians 6:17

> *For the word of God is living and active. Sharper than any double-edged sword, it penetrates even to dividing soul and spirit, joints and marrow; it judges the thoughts and attitudes of the heart.*
>
> Hebrews 4:12

This spiritual sword is an unusual weapon because it pierces your own heart. Over the years, as I have faced different challenges, I've

97

used my Bible concordance and my Bible software programs to find scriptures that touch my heart and help me fight my spiritual battles. I have written Bible verses on index cards so I could refer to them throughout the day. I did this to help me change my thinking. For example, when I'm tempted to hold a grudge, I remind myself about God's generous compassion. The scriptures remind me why I should forgive, and they set me straight about my own need for mercy and forgiveness. When I am afraid, I use scriptures that give me courage. Sometimes a scripture is a loving promise and other times a stern warning. I look for one that motivates me.

The scriptures are powerful, but their power is not some mystical force that hurts Satan. Remember that Satan even quoted scriptures to Jesus. The power of the scriptures is in how they strengthen us and help build our faith so that we do not give in to temptation. Jesus explained that the word of God is as important for the soul as food is for the body.

I remember one of my first small victories. I had heard a lesson about recognizing the spiritual battles we face in our own thoughts, and how to fight back with God's word. Shortly afterward, I was tempted to miss a church service that I regularly attended. My two young children were taking long naps, and my husband had gone ahead to a meeting. As I contemplated the challenges of getting two sleepy children up and out of the house by myself, the thought crossed my mind: "I don't want to go to church." For the first time, I saw clearly that I was in a battle with Satan in my thoughts. So I tried to think of a scripture that I could use, and Hebrews 10:25 came to mind – *"Let us not give up meeting together, as some are in the habit of doing, but let us encourage one another..."* This scripture helped me remember my convictions about the importance of church services, and that enabled me to change my attitude. I got my children up, and we went to the service.

The most rewarding part of that victory came later. As I was listening to the lesson, I realized what a great victory I had experienced. Most likely, I would have decided to go to the church service anyway, but I would have felt guilty and hypocritical for not wanting to make the effort to go. Satan would have gotten me coming and going. But instead of guilt, I was filled with peace. I had recognized Satan's scheme, engaged him in battle, and won the fight. I was experiencing the life and peace mentioned in Romans 8:6.

* * *

Another form of meditation that is extremely helpful in our spiritual battle is addressed in the following verse:

Finally, brothers, whatever is true, whatever is noble, whatever is right, whatever is pure, whatever is lovely, whatever is admirable--if anything is excellent or praiseworthy--think about such things.

Philippians 4:8

Learning to focus on good thoughts will go a long way toward helping you purify your thoughts. Kicking out an impure thought is a lot easier if you can turn your thoughts to something that is true, noble, right, pure, lovely, admirable, excellent or praiseworthy. But coming up with good things to think about is not as natural as thinking about our worries, fears or other impure thoughts. Something that helped me was to make a list of good thoughts that were true, right, pure and so forth. I began to look for examples in two areas: 1) biblical examples; and 2) modern day examples.

Biblical Examples: We have already considered how we can meditate on specific scriptures to help purify our thoughts when we are tempted, but we can also find some noble, admirable and praiseworthy stories in the Bible to inspire us. For example, if you are struggling with thoughts of low self-esteem, remembering how Jesus willingly laid down his life for you can help you feel loved. Stories of God's mighty power and his loving care can help us turn away worry and fear. The promises of God are also a source of inspiration. Thinking about God's promise of heaven can help us turn away greed and discontentment. God promises to walk with us, live with us and receive us. He promises us a rich welcome into heaven. Jesus said he will prepare a place for us in his Father's house.

<u>Modern Day Examples</u>: We can also consider modern day examples of people who have done noble, admirable and excellent deeds. For example, I know people who have made great personal sacrifices for God. Some have gone to third world countries to help the poor, and others have given up successful careers to work full time in the ministry. Still others have been great examples of openness, perseverance and faith. These inspirational deeds motivate me to be more sacrificial and faithful.

* * *

Thinking about true, noble, right, pure, lovely, admirable, excellent or praiseworthy thoughts is one of our greatest defenses. For example, when I feel irritated or impatient, I ask myself what a right or pure response would be. As soon as I consider that question, I can quickly see that my irritation is not helping me or the person with whom I am irritated. If a bitter thought about an old hurt pops into my mind, it helps me to remember that it is admirable to forgive and that we are to pray for those who mistreat us. Then if I say a quick prayer for the person who hurt me and ask God to not hold their sin against them, it has an immediate impact on my thoughts. I cannot continue to hold their sin against them if I am praying for the salvation of their soul. In a few moments, I have replaced a bitter thought with genuine concern. Over time, I have seen these old hurts fade away. God's wisdom is amazing!

If I am watchful, I can turn away an impure thought in a moment. But if I'm not thinking about how I can respond with what is admirable, true or lovely, I can easily take a more negative path. The more I have practiced purifying my thoughts, the greater success I have had and the more peace I've enjoyed. In the past, I have allowed a little impure thought to grow into a long period of discouragement or several days of disagreements with my husband. Now, I can more readily recognize Satan's schemes and can often turn away that first impure thought and not go down a destructive path. Sometimes I have to pray hard, but with God's help, I can turn away my harmful thoughts.

One impure thought has the potential to grow into a lot of heartache and sin. Our challenge is to catch it as quickly as possible and turn it away. This will take practice. The verse that immediately follows *"think about such things"* encourages us to put these things into practice.

> *Whatever you have learned or received or heard from me, or seen in me--put it into practice. And the God of peace will be with you.* [Emphasis added.]
>
> Philippians 4:9

In the worksheet that follows this chapter, there is an exercise for you to identify examples of each of these areas of good thoughts. Be sure to take the time to make a list. Choose your favorite "good" thoughts to meditate on so that you can be better prepared. The more you exercise your mind, the easier it is to quickly turn away an impure thought and the more peace you will enjoy.

Following are a few examples of the kinds of thoughts that we need to recognize as Satan's schemes. This exercise will give you a little practice in identifying Satan's scheme and making your thoughts obedient to Christ. I encourage you to take time to consider your thoughts and see specific ways you can set your mind on having pure thoughts. When you identify an impure thought, decide to give it no freedom in your mind. Then find a scripture or the inspiration to help you change your thinking. Use it daily until you see a transformation.

Giving Up: Satan has a scheme to get each one of us to give up our Christian life. He will use fears, doubts, unresolved conflicts and anything else he can think of to achieve his goal.

Thought: *You can't do this anymore. Give up.*

Meditation: What scripture in the Bible gives you strength to keep going when it is not easy?

> *. . . "No eye has seen, no ear has heard, no mind has conceived what God has prepared for those who love him . . . "*
>
> 1 Corinthians 2:9
>
> *I can do everything through him who gives me strength.*
>
> Philippians 4:13

Request to God: God, help me remember all the good things that come from you and never give up.

* * *

Marriage: If you are married, what is Satan's scheme in your marriage? Does he tempt you to be indifferent? Does he tempt you to be bitter or arrogant? What thoughts do you need to take captive regarding your marriage?

Thought: _____

If you are single, what is Satan's scheme for you in regard to your "singleness"? Are you content? Does he tempt you with impurity or immorality? What thoughts do you need to take captive?

Thought: _____

Meditation: There are many scriptures that address our devotion to God. Find one that specifically addresses your challenge. Here are a few examples:

> *Therefore what God has joined together, let man not separate.*
> Mark 10:9

> *Let us not become weary in doing good, for at the proper time we will reap a harvest if we do not give up.*
> Galatians 6:9

> *. . . I have learned to be content whatever the circumstances.*
> Philippians 4:11

Request to God:

If married: God, please help me stop thinking about ending my marriage. Help me give my heart again.

If single: Help me live for you with undivided devotion.

If single and you would like to marry some day: Help me be patient and faithful as I wait for a godly husband.

* * *

Greed: Greed is something that can contaminate our spirits. It can create a deep dissatisfaction in us, even when we are very blessed. Greed is defined as an excessive desire for getting or having more.[43] Do you struggle with thoughts prompted by greed?

Thought: _____

Meditation: What does the Bible say or what inspiration helps you overcome greed?

> *But godliness with contentment is great gain. For we brought nothing into the world, and we can take nothing out of it.*
>
> 1 Timothy 6:6-8

> *However, as it is written: "No eye has seen, no ear has heard, no mind has conceived what God has prepared for those who love him."*
>
> 1 Corinthians 2:9

Request to God: Help me be content with what I have. Help me want godliness more than anything else.

* * *

Sexually Impure Thoughts: We can struggle with a long list of sexually impure thoughts. Do you fantasize about ungodly things? How does Satan tempt you?

Thought: _____

Meditation: What scripture helps you change your thoughts when you are tempted with sexual impurity?

> *But among you <u>there must not be even a hint</u> of sexual immorality, or of any kind of impurity, or of greed, because these are improper for God's holy people.* [Emphasis added.]
>
> Ephesians 5:3

> *For of this you can be sure: No immoral, impure or greedy person--such a man is an idolater--has any inheritance in the kingdom of Christ and of God*
>
> Ephesians 5:5

> *"Therefore come out from them and be separate, says the Lord. Touch no unclean thing, and I will receive you. I will be a Father to you, and you will be my sons and daughters, says the Lord Almighty.*
>
> 2 Corinthians 6:17-18

Request to God: _____.

* * *

Bitterness: Bitterness is something that develops because of past hurts. It may be the result of a situation with a family member, an old boyfriend, neighbor or something your spouse said or did. Does Satan tempt you with bitterness or a lack of forgiveness?

Thought: _____

Meditation: What does the Bible say about it?

> *The godless in heart harbor resentment . . .*
>
> Job 36:13

> *Get rid of all bitterness, rage and anger, brawling and slander, along with every form of malice. Be kind and compassionate to one another, forgiving each other, just as in Christ God forgave you.*
>
> Ephesians 4:31-32

> *. . . bless those who curse you, pray for those who mistreat you.*
>
> Luke 6:28

Request to God: Help me forgive this old hurt from my heart. Help me remember how much forgiveness you have given me. Please do not hold this sin against them.

* * *

Learning to purify our thoughts is one of our greatest and most rewarding inner beauty treatments. Remember that purity is a "get to" not a "have to." Like enjoying pure water or pure air, purifying our thoughts is a wonderful blessing from God. Take time to consider your thoughts, confess those that are impure, find scriptures that give you strength and spend quality time in prayer. I don't want to give the impression that this is an easy 1-2-3 process, because it isn't. It is a spiritual battle that each one of us must fight, but the victories will be well worth the effort. Let's be faithful and determined to purify our thoughts.

Worksheet 9 - Pure Thoughts

1. What are Satan's schemes in your life? When do you struggle the most in your thoughts?

2. List several examples of inspirational thoughts in each of the following categories. (You can find more examples of these in the group study guide on my website under "Free Resources")

True thoughts:

"Never will I leave you; never will I forsake you." (Hebrews 13:5)

Noble thoughts:

. . . pray for those who mistreat you. (Luke 6:28)

Right thoughts:

... for man's anger does not bring about the righteous life that God desires. (James 1:20)

Pure thoughts:

But godliness with contentment is great gain. (1 Timothy 6:6)

Lovely thoughts:

The Lord is gracious and compassionate, slow to anger and rich in love. (Psalm 145:8)

Admirable thoughts:

Greater love has no one than this, that he lay down his life for his friends. (John 15:13)

Excellent thoughts:

I can do everything through him who gives me strength. (Philippians 4:13)

Praiseworthy thoughts:

For God so loved the world that he gave his one and only Son. (John 3:16a)

3. Make a list of the thoughts that you want to purify. Then find a scripture or a source of inspiration that helps you change your thinking.

– Chapter 10 –

Pure Words

Evil words are ugly and incredibly destructive. They can be biting, hateful, cruel, slanderous or full of anger. Our words reveal a lot about our inner beauty, or the lack thereof, because they come straight from the heart:

> *The good man brings good things out of the good stored up in his heart, and the evil man brings evil things out of the evil stored up in his heart. <u>For out of the overflow of his heart his mouth speaks</u>.* [Emphasis added.]
>
> Luke 6:45

This chapter is entitled "Pure Words," but it is really the beginning of a study of how we can purify our hearts. The words we speak are the best indicators of what is going on in our hearts. The following verse warns us about the consequences of careless words:

> *If anyone considers himself religious and yet does not keep a tight rein on his tongue, he deceives himself and his religion is worthless.*
>
> James 1:26

Our religion does us no good if we don't watch what we say. We continually need to purify our speech. New Christians may find that they need to be more truthful or to stop coarse joking. Those who have been Christians for years may face less obvious challenges. Perhaps their struggle is with bitter words, critical words or words driven by pride. The following are several areas of speech that the Bible addresses:

Slander

The following verses specifically address women:

> *Likewise, teach the older women to be reverent in the way they live, not to be slanderers [diabolos] or addicted to much wine, but to teach what is good.*

Titus 2:3

> *In the same way, their wives are to be women worthy of respect, not malicious talkers [diabolos] but temperate and trustworthy in everything.*

1 Timothy 3:11

Definition: *Diabolos* (dee-ab´-ol-os); a traducer; especially Satan; false accuser, devil, slanderer.[44]

The word traducer means someone who says untrue or malicious things about another person; one who defames, slanders or vilifies. Slander means the utterance in the presence of another person of a false statement or statements that are damaging to a third person's character or reputation.[45] The Greek word *diabolos* is translated "Satan" thirty-four times in the Bible.[46] Satan is our accuser (Revelation 12:10), and he uses his words to deceive and destroy us.

The following verse shows how God uses his words to strengthen us.

> *. . . the God who gives life to the dead and calls things that are not as though they were.*

Romans 4:17

God called Gideon a mighty warrior, and Jesus called Peter a rock. Both of these men lived up to their new names. However, just as positive words can call people higher, negative words can discourage or destroy them. The words we use can have a powerful effect on those around us.

> *The tongue has the power of life and death, and those who love it will eat its fruit.*

Proverbs 18:21

110

How easy it is to say something negative or voice an opinion that puts someone in a bad light. These easily spoken words can deeply hurt someone. And we cannot slander someone and live a blameless life:

> *LORD, who may dwell in your sanctuary? Who may live on your holy hill? He whose walk is blameless and who does what is righteous, who speaks the truth from his heart and has no slander on his tongue, who does his neighbor no wrong and casts no slur on his fellowman . . .*
>
> Psalms 15:1-3

Gossip

Gossip can be appealing because it has an effect of connecting us to others. It can give us a sense of belonging when we would otherwise feel like an outsider. Even if we believe it is wrong and intend never to gossip, we can find ourselves in a conversation full of gossip. Not wanting to participate, yet not wanting to be excluded, is certainly a difficult position. If you choose not to gossip, you may not only be excluded, but may also be the focus of more gossip.

Gossip is a pet sin of the world. Many magazines, television shows and web blogs are rooted in gossip. Gossip is clearly an example of the choice we have to be a friend of the world or a friend of God (James 4:4). We need to understand how harmful gossip is.

> *A gossip betrays a confidence; so avoid a man who talks too much.*
>
> Proverbs 20:19

> *A perverse man stirs up dissension, and a gossip separates close friends.*
>
> Proverbs 16:28

> *The words of a gossip are like choice morsels; they go down to a man's inmost parts.*
>
> Proverbs 26:22

Your innermost part is your heart. Something that seems as small as a little gossip can seriously corrupt your heart. It can turn you against another person and destroy a relationship that had previously been very close. Gossip is dangerous.

Complaining and Arguing

Do everything without complaining or arguing, so that you may become blameless and pure . . .

Philippians 2:14-15

Although complaining and arguing can seem harmless, both are impure and have a negative impact on those around us. We are warned that we will be held accountable for our words:

"But I tell you that men will have to give account on the day of judgment for every careless word they have spoken. For by your words you will be acquitted, and by your words you will be condemned."

Matthew 12:36-37

Our words have spiritual consequences, so we should carefully consider what we say. Impure words of any kind create problems in our relationships with each other as well as our relationship with God. The following are more examples of the kinds of words we are called to purify:

Lying and Deceit

Reckless words pierce like a sword, but the tongue of the wise brings healing. Truthful lips endure forever, but a lying tongue lasts only a moment.

Proverbs 12:18-19

The tongue that brings healing is a tree of life, but a deceitful tongue crushes the spirit.

Proverbs 15:4

Coarse Joking and Foolish Talk

But among you there must not be even a hint of sexual immorality, or of any kind of impurity, or of greed, because these are improper for God's holy people. Nor should there be obscenity, foolish talk or coarse joking, which are out of place, but rather thanksgiving. [Emphasis added.]

Ephesians 5:3-4

Anger and Rage

A fool gives full vent to his anger, but a wise man keeps himself under control.

Proverbs 29:11

Get rid of all bitterness, rage and anger, brawling and slander, along with every form of malice.

Ephesians 4:31

Filthy Language

But now you must rid yourselves of all such things as these: anger, rage, malice, slander, and filthy language from your lips.

Colossians 3:8

Swearing

Above all, my brothers, do not swear--not by heaven or by earth or by anything else. Let your "Yes" be yes, and your "No," no, or you will be condemned.

James 5:12

Cursing

Bless those who persecute you; bless and do not curse.

Romans 12:14

If a man curses his father or mother, his lamp will be snuffed out in pitch darkness.

Proverbs 20:20

Too Many Words

The more the words, the less the meaning, and how does that profit anyone?

Ecclesiastes 6:11

When words are many, sin is not absent, but he who holds his tongue is wise.

Proverbs 10:19

* * *

Our words have a far-reaching impact and can change the course of our lives:

Likewise the tongue is a small part of the body, but it makes great boasts. Consider what a great forest is set on fire by a small spark. The tongue also is a fire, a world of evil among the parts of the body. It corrupts the whole person, sets the whole course of his life on fire, and is itself set on fire by hell.

All kinds of animals, birds, reptiles and creatures of the sea are being tamed and have been tamed by man, but no man can tame the tongue. It is a restless evil, full of deadly poison.

With the tongue we praise our Lord and Father, and with it we curse men, who have been made in God's likeness. Out of the same mouth come praise and cursing. My brothers, this should not be.

James 3:5-12

This scripture gives us a clear picture of the impact of only a few words. Just like a spark in a forest, our words can launch a sequence of events that we cannot control. Yet, we are told that we cannot tame the tongue. So you may be wondering, "What does God expect me to do?" Let's consider again what Jesus said about our words:

The good man brings good things out of the good stored up in his heart, and the evil man brings evil things out of the evil stored up in his heart. For out of the overflow of his heart his mouth speaks.

Luke 6:45

You cannot tame the tongue, so the words you speak will reveal whatever is in your heart. However, this does not mean that you have no control or that there is no solution. To change something about your speech, your solution is to work on your heart. If something comes out of your mouth that is not pleasing to God, you need to examine what is going on in your heart.

If I am irritated about something that is happening around me, my words will likely show my irritation. I may be able to hide it for a while, but eventually it will come out in my words or my lack of words. But if I get rid of the irritation in my heart, I don't have to worry about saying something that's hurtful.

It is tempting to blame others for my impure words. It is easy to think, "If they had not made me angry, I would not have said it." But the words that I speak come from *my* heart, and I am the one who is responsible for them.

We must learn to dig out the sin in our own hearts. What's in my heart when I speak angry, hurtful words? Is it pride? Is it hatred? Am I insecure? Why did I slander this person? What is driving me when I gossip? Is it people-pleasing or trying to gain power or influence? We need to carefully consider the things that are going on inside our hearts. Then we can work on the source of our impure words and be much more successful in our efforts to purify our words.

God tells us that our hearts can change:

> *Rid yourselves of all the offenses you have committed, and get a new heart and a new spirit. Why will you die, O house of Israel?*
>
> Ezekiel 18:31

> *I will give you a new heart and put a new spirit in you; I will remove from you your heart of stone and give you a heart of flesh.*
>
> Ezekiel 36:26

> *Those whom I love I rebuke and discipline. So be earnest, and repent.*
>
> Revelation 3:19

God calls us to be earnest and repent when we see sin in our hearts. It may take days of fasting and prayer, but remember that God wants to help us change our hearts. He even offers to give us a new heart. How amazing that is! God helps us in every way. Our part is to humbly turn to him.

* * *

The scriptures also give us direction on the kinds of words that are helpful:

> *Do not let any unwholesome talk come out of your mouths, but only <u>what is helpful for building others up according to their needs</u>, that it may benefit those who listen.* [Emphasis added.]
>
> Ephesians 4:29

> *<u>A gentle answer</u> turns away wrath, but a harsh word stirs up anger.* [Emphasis added.]
>
> Proverbs 15:1

> *Do not repay evil with evil or insult with insult, <u>but with blessing</u>, because to this you were called so that you may inherit a blessing. For, "Whoever would love life and see good days must keep his tongue from evil and his lips from deceitful speech."* [Emphasis added.]
>
> 1 Peter 3:9-10

Pleasant words are a honeycomb, sweet to the soul and healing to the bones. [Emphasis added.]

Proverbs 16:24

Instead, speaking the truth in love, we will in all things grow up into him who is the Head, that is, Christ. [Emphasis added.]

Ephesians 4:15

Therefore encourage one another and build each other up, just as in fact you are doing.

1 Thessalonians 5:11

. . . give thanks in all circumstances, for this is God's will for you in Christ Jesus. [Emphasis added.]

1 Thessalonians 5:18

Through Jesus, therefore, let us continually offer to God a sacrifice of praise--the fruit of lips that confess his name. [Emphasis added.]

Hebrews 13:15

Our words wield a lot of power. They can heal or destroy. It is no wonder that the Bible contains so many scriptures that instruct us about our speech. If you are challenged in a specific area of speech, take the time to consider what the Bible has to say and examine what is going on in your heart. To be a true Christian, you must keep a tight rein on your tongue (James 1:26).

May the words of my mouth and the meditation of my heart be pleasing in your sight, O LORD, my Rock and my Redeemer.

Psalms 19:14

Worksheet 10 - Pure Words

1. Consider each area of speech from the previous pages: slander, gossip, complaining, arguing, lying, deceit, coarse joking, foolish talk, anger, rage, filthy language, swearing, and cursing. In which of these areas do you see evidence of a need to control your words?

_____

_____

_____

2. What's in your heart that causes these words to come out of your mouth?

_____

_____

_____

3. Consider again the scriptures describing the kinds of words we should speak. Which of these are your strengths? In which areas would you like to improve?

_____

_____

_____

_____

_____

_____

_____

Memory Verse: Psalms 19:14

– Chapter 11 –

A Pure Heart

Blessed are the pure in heart, for they will see God.
Matthew 5:8

Our most important goal in our pursuit of purity is having a pure heart. God promises that the pure in heart will see him. This meeting will be so magnificent – it will be far beyond anything we will have ever experienced or can even imagine. Whatever it takes to purify our hearts will be worth it.

> *However, as it is written: "No eye has seen, no ear has heard, no mind has conceived what God has prepared for those who love him."*
> 1 Corinthians 2:9

Throughout the previous chapters, we have considered the impact our hearts have on our motives, sexual purity, words, thoughts and even our fashion choices. Our hearts impact everything we do. Now, we have finally drilled down to the most important area of purity. There is so much we can learn about our hearts from the scriptures. Remember that the scriptures are our spiritual mirror. Let's look carefully as we consider how we can purify our hearts.

Wholeheartedness

The first step to purifying our hearts is to be wholehearted in our relationship with God. In fact, you cannot find God unless you search for him with your whole heart:

> *"For I know the plans I have for you," declares the Lord, "plans to prosper you and not to harm you, plans to give you hope and a future. Then you will call upon me and come and pray to me, and I will listen to you. <u>You will seek me and find me when you seek me with all your heart.</u>"* [Emphasis added.]
>
> Jeremiah 29:11-13

Wholehearted devotion to God is the foundation of our relationship with him. Jesus explained in his famous sermon on the mountainside why we must give God our whole heart:

> *"No one can serve two masters. Either he will hate the one and love the other, or he will be devoted to the one and despise the other. You cannot serve both God and Money.*
>
> Matthew 6:24

We can love more than two people at the same time, but loving two people is different from serving two masters. A master is one who rules over you and determines how you live your life. Trying to make two masters happy would be a burden – and impossible. Eventually, you will have to choose between the two, and give your allegiance to one over the other. Our allegiance and love for God are shown by our obedience to him.

> *This is love for God: to obey his commands. And his commands are not burdensome.*
>
> 1 John 5:3

If you want to show God your wholehearted devotion, you will obey his commands. You will look at the areas where it is most difficult for you to obey, and figure out why. Do his commands feel burdensome? If so, this is a warning sign that you are giving your heart somewhere else.

A Deceitful Heart

> *The heart is deceitful above all things and beyond cure. Who can understand it?*
>
> Jeremiah 17:9

We can believe something deep down in our hearts and still be wrong! The first example of a deceived heart is when Eve believed Satan's lie (Genesis 3:4). Her deceived heart told her not to trust God, so she took things into her own hands and disobeyed God. Just like Eve, we can also be deceived.

> *But I am afraid that just as Eve was deceived by the serpent's cunning, your minds may somehow be led astray from your sincere and pure devotion to Christ.*
>
> 2 Corinthians 11:3

Satan tries to deceive us in many ways. He is a liar and a deceiver.

> *You belong to your father, the devil, and you want to carry out your father's desire. He was a murderer from the beginning, not holding to the truth, for there is no truth in him. When he lies, he speaks his native language, for he is a liar and the father of lies.*
>
> John 8:44

> *The great dragon was hurled down--that ancient serpent called the devil, or Satan, <u>who leads the whole world astray</u>. He was hurled to the earth, and his angels with him.* [Emphasis added.]
>
> Revelation 12:9

Satan is always working to deceive us, and he is an expert. He can make something dangerous look appealing, and make something that is perverse look fun. He is the father of lies, and he tells us lies every day.

There are several ways that we can protect ourselves from deception. One is by daily contact with other Christians. When we stay close to each other, it is much harder for Satan to deceive us.

> *But encourage one another daily, as long as it is called Today, so that none of you may be hardened by sin's deceitfulness.*
>
> Hebrews 3:13

Another way we can protect our hearts is by prayer, openness and meditation. The Bible will help us discern the attitudes of our hearts and see spiritual truths more clearly (Hebrews 4:12). We can examine a feeling and let the scriptures help us determine if we are deceived. For example, I have justified holding onto old hurts. But reading that the godless in heart harbor resentment (Job 36:13) helped me realize that I was deceived. I felt justified and *godly*, but I was actually *godless*. This scripture helped me see the truth and begin to change my heart.

Remember that Satan works hard to deceive you, but with the help of the scriptures, you can overcome his deceptions:

> *The coming of the lawless one will be in accordance with the work of Satan displayed in all kinds of counterfeit miracles, signs and wonders, and in every sort of evil that deceives those who are perishing. <u>They perish because they refused to love the truth</u> and so be saved.* [Emphasis added.]
>
> 2 Thessalonians 2:9-10

> *To the Jews who had believed him, Jesus said, "If you hold to my teaching, you are really my disciples. Then you will know the truth, and the truth will set you free."*
>
> John 8:31-32

Loving the truth is not always easy, because the truth can hurt sometimes. But not loving the truth will cost us everything.

* * *

A Secretive Heart

> *If we had forgotten the name of our God or spread out our hands to a foreign god, would not God have discovered it, since he knows the secrets of the heart?*
>
> Psalms 44:20-21

> *For God will bring every deed into judgment, including every hidden thing, whether it is good or evil.*
>
> Ecclesiastes 12:14

God is always searching our hearts (Jeremiah 17:10), and he knows all our secrets. He knows hidden sin will destroy us.

> *"Woe to you, teachers of the law and Pharisees, you hypocrites! You are like whitewashed tombs, which look beautiful on the outside but on the inside are full of dead men's bones and everything unclean."*
>
> Matthew 23:27

A whitewashed tomb is a good picture of hidden sin – pretty on the outside, but entirely unclean on the inside. Some of the sins we can try to hide in our hearts are pride, lust, hatred, malice, envy, jealousy, anger, greed, idolatry, selfish ambition and deceit. To overcome the secretive heart that is associated with these sins, we have to be open and humble. Coming into the light (confessing sin) is the solution for a secretive heart.

> *"This is the verdict: Light has come into the world, but men loved darkness instead of light because their deeds were evil. Everyone who does evil hates the light, and will not come into the light for fear that his deeds will be exposed. <u>But whoever lives by the truth comes into the light,</u> so that it may be seen plainly that what he has done has been done through God."* [Emphasis added.]
>
> John 3:19-21

> *Therefore confess your sins to each other and pray for each other so that you may be healed. The prayer of a righteous man is powerful and effective.*
>
> James 5:16

Note: There are secrets that we can and should keep. Jesus explains in the following verse:

> *"Be careful not to do your 'acts of righteousness' before men, to be seen by them. If you do, you will have no reward from your Father in heaven. So when you give to the needy, do not announce it with trumpets, as the hypocrites do in the synagogues and on the streets, to be honored by men. I tell you the truth, they have received their reward in full. But when you give to the needy, do not let your left hand know what your right hand is doing, so that your giving may be in secret. Then your Father, who sees what is done in secret, will reward you."*
>
> Matthew 6:1-4

The only secret we should keep is the good we do. So be open about your shortcomings and keep your good deeds to yourself. Our natural tendency is to do just the opposite, but doing it God's way will help us stay humble and protect our hearts.

* * *

An Unbelieving Heart

> *See to it, brothers, that none of you has a sinful, unbelieving heart that turns away from the living God.*
>
> Hebrews 3:12

And without faith it is impossible to please God, because any-one who comes to him must believe that he exists and that he rewards those who earnestly seek him.

Hebrews 11:6

We typically think of an unbeliever as a non-Christian; however, these scriptures were written to Christians. Remaining faithful and wholehearted throughout life is one of our greatest challenges. We can have a strong faith for a long time, but then suddenly find ourselves struggling with a lack of faith. We may not even know how it happened. Symptoms include not praying, not studying the scriptures, not obeying the scriptures and not being open about sin.

Even strong Christians can have areas of unbelief that they must work through. For example, Elijah displayed great faith when he challenged the 450 prophets of Baal, but ran away when the queen threatened his life. God helped him to find the strength to overcome his faithlessness (1 Kings 18-19). We must take any area of faithlessness in our lives very seriously, because it can get to the point that our faith is destroyed.

Timothy, my son, I give you this instruction in keeping with the prophecies once made about you, so that by following them you may fight the good fight, holding on to faith and a good conscience. Some have rejected these and so have shipwrecked their faith. [Emphasis added.]

1 Timothy 1:18-19

Our faith is tested in many ways. We must remember that this is a good thing – our faith is more precious than gold (1 Peter 1:7). When God refines us through trials, he is helping us gain something of great value. Abraham is an example of someone whose faith grew as he went through his trials.

Against all hope, Abraham in hope believed and so became the father of many nations, just as it had been said to him, "So shall your offspring be." Without weakening in his faith, he faced the fact that his body was as good as dead--since he was about a hundred years old--and that Sarah's womb was also dead. Yet he did not waver through unbelief regarding the promise of

God, <u>but was strengthened in his faith</u> and gave glory to God,
being fully persuaded that God had power to do what he had
promised. [Emphasis added.]

Romans 4:18-21

Abraham's trials strengthened his faith. We too need to seek more
faith as we go through our trials. Satan has many schemes that are designed to weaken our faith, but God's purpose in our trials is to help
us develop more faith. Our goal must be to grow in our faith more and
more because we do not know what challenge lies ahead.

A Hard Heart

They are darkened in their understanding and separated from
the life of God because of the ignorance that is in them due to
the hardening of their hearts. Having lost all sensitivity, they
have given themselves over to sensuality so as to indulge in
every kind of impurity, with a continual lust for more.

Ephesians 4:18-19

Our hearts harden when we sin. This is true for both Christians and
non-Christians. The result of a hard heart is spiritual ignorance and the
loss of our sensitivity to what is right and wrong. Another symptom of
a hard heart is that we cannot see or hear spiritual truths.

For this people's heart has become calloused; they hardly hear
with their ears, and they have closed their eyes. Otherwise they
might see with their eyes, hear with their ears, understand with
their hearts and turn, and I would heal them.

Acts 28:27

One specific sin that hardens our hearts is pride. The following
verse describes what happened to the powerful King Nebuchadnezzar:

But when his heart became arrogant and hardened with pride,
he was deposed from his royal throne and stripped of his glory.

Daniel 5:20

Hardness of heart is a frightening heart condition, because hard-
hearted or prideful persons have a distorted view of their need for
God. And a hard heart does not respond to spiritual input. However,
there is still hope because God has the power to humble us. Nebuchadnezzar learned this lesson.

Now I, Nebuchadnezzar, praise and exalt and glorify the King of heaven, because everything he does is right and all his ways are just. And those who walk in pride he is able to humble.
[Emphasis added.]

Daniel 4:37

God humbles us in different ways. Sometimes he humbles us through his love. Feeling God's love can be a very humbling experience. Another way he humbles us is through discipline. Nebuchadnezzar is an example of someone who was humbled by God's discipline. God can humble a prideful heart, but a better solution is to learn to humble ourselves (James 4:10; 1 Peter 5:5-6). This is something we can learn to do. It just takes practice – seek advice about your life, be open about the things you are ashamed of, and pray like David did in the following scriptures:

Search me, O God, and know my heart; test me and know my anxious thoughts. See if there is any offensive way in me, and lead me in the way everlasting.

Psalms 139:23-24

Create in me a pure heart, O God, and renew a steadfast spirit within me.

Psalms 51:10

We should all pray this prayer often. There is nothing more important than a pure heart:

Above all else, guard your heart, for it is the wellspring of life.
Proverbs 4:23

A wellspring is the source of a stream or underground well. In the same way, your heart is what fills up your life. It overflows into all the areas of your life: your sexual purity, your choice of clothing, what you do for entertainment, your words and your thoughts. Your purity in all of these areas is rooted in your heart. That's why we should guard our hearts above all else.

Purifying our hearts is a lifetime pursuit. Sarah and Naomi are examples of older women who were still purifying their hearts in their old age. Sarah had to purify her unbelieving heart. She scoffed at the thought of having a baby in her old age, but she learned that nothing

126

was too hard for the Lord (Genesis 18:12-14). Naomi struggled with a bitter heart, but found that God had not stopped showing her kindness (Ruth 1:20; 2:20). Both Sarah and Naomi held on to their faith and fought their battles for a pure heart.

We must do the same thing. No matter how old we are or how long we have been a Christian, we must continue to purify our hearts. Purity protects us and insulates us from many troubles of the world. Impurity, on the other hand, is a dangerous threat. It hardens our hearts and distorts our view of spiritual truths.

God offers us an amazing opportunity when he calls us to purify ourselves. Take the time to make your heart beautiful to God. Beauty treatments of the heart include wholeheartedness, honesty, openness, faithfulness, humility, contentment, submission and trust. Make these a part of your spiritual beauty routine so you can become more and more beautiful to God.

Remember that purity is God's gift to us. Only through his word, his Holy Spirit and his amazing sacrifice for our sins can we enjoy any purity at all. Purity is a privilege, and we honor God every time we purify a part of our lives. Let's make ourselves beautiful to God, and give him all the glory as we enjoy the power and privilege of purity.

> *It is God who arms me with strength and makes my way perfect.*
> *He makes my feet like the feet of a deer; he enables me to stand*
> *on the heights.*
>
> Psalms 18:32-33

Worksheet 11 - A Pure Heart

1. In what ways do you guard your heart?

2. What is your greatest challenge in having a pure heart?

3. Do you have areas of unbelief in your heart? If so, what are they?

4. How do you fight pride in your heart?

Memory Verse: Proverbs 4:23

– Chapter 12 –

Protecting Our Daughters

Then they can train the younger women . . . to be self-controlled and pure . . .

Titus 2:4-5

I would like to share a few thoughts about the challenges we face to teach our daughters about purity. In these times, passing on the truth about the privilege of purity is not an easy task. Our children have more access to the world than I could have imagined during my childhood. Over the last several decades, statistics show an increase in STDs, drug and alcohol abuse, self-mutilation, suicide and violence among teens, and provide alarming evidence of the special challenges our teens face as they are exposed to more and more worldliness.

Teens are exposed to things far too worldly for them to process. Impurity and sin takes a toll on any heart, young or old, but young hearts have some special challenges as they embrace impurity. Recently, on my way home from work, I sat beside a group of young teen girls on the commuter train. They had spent the day in the city and were on their way home. They unabashedly discussed going to parties and "making out" with boys. The apparent level of impurity in their lives made me sad. I thought about the impact this would have on their lives in the future and how they were seemingly unaware of the pitfalls they were facing. To them this was a "normal" part of growing up. The following quote from *Why the Sexualization of Childhood Is Harmful for Children* explains how the focus on sexuality impacts children:

It is not the fact that children are learning about sex when they are young that is a problem, the problem is what today's sexualized environment is teaching them. Children's ideas about what it means to be a boy and girl and about the nature of sex and sexuality develop gradually and are greatly influenced by the information the environment provides. The popular culture of today bombards girls with large doses of sexual content that they cannot understand and that can even scare them. It provides them with a very narrow definition of femaleness and sexuality that focuses them primarily on appearance. Their value is determined by how well they succeed at meeting the sexualized ideal. It can also promote precocious sexual behavior before they have an understanding of the deeper meanings of the behavior. When children are young, long before they can fully understand the meaning of sex and sexual relations, we should be laying the foundation for later healthy sexual relationships. And unless we begin to deal more proactively with the disconnect between what children need and what they are getting today, it does not bode well for the future of intimate and caring relationships in which sex is a part, when today's children grow up.[47]

Counteracting today's sexualized environment presents parents with difficult challenges. You try to teach your daughter godly values, but movies and television shows promote premarital sex as a normal part of growing up. And many of these shows make their message appealing and make adults look disconnected and out of touch.

Another worldly appeal we parents must counteract is the pull our daughters feel to follow in the footsteps of their favorite stars. The following *Chicago Tribune* article shows how young girls can be influenced by movie stars many years older:

Multiple posters of Disney teen queen Hilary Duff decorate the bedroom of my 7-year-old daughter, a "Lizzie McGuire" fan going way back to when she was 6. There's sweet smiling Hil in the pink sweater. There's butter-haired Hil looking over her shoulder. There's Hil with the sleeveless top and choker necklace.

These are the welcomed Hilarys, the ones who evoke the Disney Channel's hit show (2001-2004), featuring the likable, effervescent junior high student, her two best friends, clueless parents and a bratty little brother. Lizzie's high jinks at home and school made her – and Duff – an idol for tweeners and pretweens like my daughter, Anika.

But now there's a new Hil, one whom oglers might call Hil-a-*ray, baby,* she of the knowing look, smoldering eyes, hollowed-out cheeks and exposed cleavage. This Hil is gazing upon my daughter, and my daughter is gazing right back. I do not want this Hilary in my house.[48]

Right before her own eyes, this mom is seeing the transformation of her young daughter's favorite TV star. Hollywood has a formula for building the careers of girl stars like Britney Spears, Lindsay Lohan and Hilary Duff. They market to young fans of the Disney Channel and other children's networks, and then when these stars turn 18, they pull these young fans along with an older version of their favorite star. It is a marketing ploy that brings in big bucks. What little girl doesn't want to dress like a star, sing like a star, or dance like a star! Meanwhile their "star" is on her way to becoming the next sex symbol in Hollywood.

Several years ago I had a discussion with a neighbor about her plans to take her young daughter to a Britney Spears concert. It was the year that Britney turned 18. I was surprised that she took her young daughter to this concert, but her daughter really wanted to go. After the concert, my neighbor was a little concerned about all the provocative dance moves her young daughter was doing. This mom had been duped by the Hollywood marketing campaign that was aimed directly at her young daughter.

The *Trib* article went on to say:

"Most parents say, she's just changing her image, she's sexy now," says Dr. Don Shifrin, chairman of the American Academy of Pediatrics committee on communications, which puts out policy statements on children and the media. "It's like air pollution that we don't notice until we're choking." And whether the "pollution" is coming from Hollywood or Madison Avenue, there's no way to censor the media, Shifrin says. So parents must filter media.

Liz Perle, editor in chief of Common Sense Media, an organization that helps families make media choices, agrees. "There's a heavy burden on parents to manage the messaging," she says. "You can no longer just let them see their idols go through these moments unattended. You can't cover their eyes, so we have to teach them . . . "

Children can be very accepting of their parents' reasoning, Perle says, however, "they also are going to push back. But you need to say: 'I don't think she is a good role model for you.'"

Media critic Jean Kilbourne, author of the book "So Sexy So Soon: The Sexualization of Childhood," says keeping your child safe from images that are taken from "the world of pornography" is paramount. "You do your best to make her understand, and if she doesn't understand you, take [the poster] down. It's the same as if she put an Absolut vodka poster on her wall. You'd take it down."[49]

* * *

Times may have changed, but the challenges we face as parents to guide our children are not new. A Biblical example is the story of Dinah, Jacob's only daughter (Genesis 34). When she visited the women of the nearby city, she was raped by a man whose father ruled the area. Two of her brothers retaliated by murdering all the men in the city. Then the family was forced to move. Years later, when Jacob was about to die, he refused to bless his two sons because of their violent behavior. Instead, they received a curse (Genesis 49:5-7).

The results of Dinah's tragedy unfolded over a period of years. The tragedy in the life of a young girl who has been violated can go on for a long time – even a lifetime. And it not only affects the girl herself, it also affects her family.

I want to know how this happened to Dinah. Why did her family allow her to go unchaperoned to this city? Did they think this pagan community was safe? Did they let her go because she insisted she could take care of herself? There are a lot of unanswered questions in this story. Perhaps this was an isolated case of bad judgment on behalf of her parents. Maybe they had been lulled into a sense of security in an unsafe place.

This is a story of rape, but other less violent events and behaviors can have long lasting consequences in a young girl's life. When young hearts are exposed to large doses of the world, there can be serious consequences. These consequences include eating disorders, cutting oneself, promiscuity, drugs and alcohol abuse. Many of these problems are a result of the overload of sexual content in young girls' lives. Teens (both our sons and daughters) face many assaults on their purity. We need to make sure that we do not let it happen just because it is acceptable in our culture. We cannot let the world define what is or is not safe for our children.

Protecting our children is possible. We must teach them how to protect their own hearts and how to fight their own spiritual battles. We should start early by restricting their access to worldly television shows that are inappropriate for young children. As they grow, we can give them a positive view of purity, and help them see the heartaches experienced by people who do not follow God. We can also give them the example of our own lives and how God has blessed us as we have purified ourselves. Let's pass on God's love and blessings to our children.

> *These commandments that I give you today are to be upon your hearts. Impress them on your children. Talk about them when you sit at home and when you walk along the road, when you lie down and when you get up.*
>
> Deuteronomy 6:6-7

Worksheet 12 - Protecting Our Daughters

1. Do you have a daughter or granddaughter? What are some of the challenges that she faces to be pure?

_____

_____

_____

_____

_____

_____

2. If you are a teen, what are the greatest challenges you face to live a pure life?

_____

_____

_____

_____

_____

_____

_____

_____

_____

_____

_____

Memory Verse: Deuteronomy 6:6-7

ENDNOTES:

1.   "Spiritual Progress Hard to Find in 2003," (http://www.barna.org/Flex-Page.aspx?Page=BarnaUpdate&BarnaUpdateID=155/, 2003).

2.   CNN.com/Science & Space (http://www.cnn.com/2003/TECH/space/07/22/stars.survey/) posted July 23, 2003.

3.   Dr. Nancy Etcoff, Dr. Susie Orbach, Dr. Jennifer Scott, and Heidi D'Agostino, "The Real Truth About Beauty: A Global Report," (http://www.campaignforrealbeauty.com/uploadedfiles/dove_white_paper_final.pdf, 2004), pp. 2, 10, 11.

4.   Webster's New World Dictionary Third College Edition (New York, New York: Simon & Schuster, Inc., 1988), p. 122.

5.   W. E. Vine, *Vine's Expository Dictionary of Old and New Testament Words* (Tarrytown, NY: Fleming H. Revell Company), [Bible Explorer 4.0].

6.   Ibid.

7.   Ibid.

8.   Ibid.

9.   James Strong, *Strong's Exhaustive Concordance* (Nashville, Tennessee: Crusade Bible Publishers, Inc.), [Bible Explorer 4.0].

10.   Virginia Lefler, *A Gentle & Quiet Spirit* (Grayslake, Illinois: Silverday Press, 2006), pp. 10-13.

11.   Vine.

12.   Lefler, pp.5-7.

13.   Strong.

14.   John L. Jeffcoat III, "English Bible History" (http://www.greatsite.com/timeline-english-bible-history/, 2002).

15.   Etcoff, Orbach, Scott and D'Agostino, p. 40.

16.   Herbert Lockyer, *All the Women of the Bible* (Grand Rapids, Michigan: Zondervan Publishing House, 1946), p. 14.

17.   Strong.

18.   Webster's, p. 871.

19.   Ibid, p. 359.

20.   Vine.

21.   Webster's, p. 1232.

22.   Vine.

23.   Webster's, p. 1079

24.   Wikipedia, (http://en.wikipedia.org/wiki/Trickle-down_effect).

25.   About.com/Eating Disorders (http://eatingdisorders.about.com/od/eatingdisordersinmales/a/olderwomen.htm), June 17, 2008.

26.   Robert Jamieson, A. R. Fausset, and David Brown, *Jamieson-Fausset-Brown Bible Commentary* (http://www.studylight.org/com/jfb/view.cgi?book=es&chapter=002).

27. "The Production Code" (http://en.wikipedia.org/wiki/Hays_Code., 1930).

28. Patricia M. Jones, "TV Terror," *Chicago Tribune*, October 18, 2005, Tempo Section, p. 1.

29. Internet Filter Review (http://internet-filter-review.toptenreviews.com/internet-pornography-statistics.html) September, 2003.

30. Ibid.

31. Vine.

32. "Sexually Transmitted Diseases, General Information," Centers for Disease Control (http://www.cdc.gov/nchstp/dstd/disease_info.htm), 2004.

33. Avert Global HIV/AIDS estimates, end of 2005 (http://www.avert.org/worldstats.htm), 2005.

34. National Right to Life (http://www.nrlc.org/abortion/facts/abortionstats.html).

35. "Genital HPV Infection - CDC Fact Sheet," Centers for Disease Control (http://www.cdc.gov/std/HPV/STDFact-HPV.htm), 2004.

36. Ipsos BookTrends, Book Industry Study Group and American Bookseller Association reports (https://www.rwanational.org), 2004.

37. Strong.

38. The National Library of Medicine, Medline Plus (http://www.nlm.nih.gov/medlineplus/ency/article/002473.htm#Symptoms).

39. Strong.

40. Ibid.

41. James L. Lefler, *The Complete Guide to Grace* (Downers Grove, Illinois: Silverday Press, 2008), p. 120.

42. Webster's, p 842.

43. Ibid, p 591.

44. Strong.

45. Webster's, p 1259.

46. Vine.

47. Diane Levin, Ph.D., "So Sexy, So Soon: The Sexualization of Childhood in Commercial Culture" (http://www.commercialexploitation.com/articles/4thsummit/levin.htm).

48. Maria Mooshil, "Lizzie Shows Sexy Sizzle" *Chicago Tribune*, February 21, 2006, Sec. 5, p. 1.

49. Ibid, p. 7.

The Complete
Guide *to* Grace

By James L. Lefler

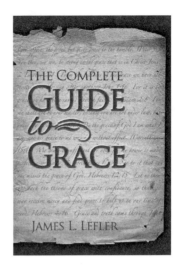

A clear understanding of God's grace is empowering, but explanations of grace often do more to muddy the water than clarify the meaning. The words grace, mercy and salvation are used interchangeably in ways inconsistent with the original Hebrew and Greek. Frequently grace is defined as unmerited favor; however, when we focus on how unworthy we are to receive it, we make it more about us than about God and risk missing the full impact of his favor.

The Complete Guide to Grace is a refreshing, motivating and comprehensive study that clears up misconceptions about grace. It reveals foundational truths about grace, mercy and forgiveness that can radically change your life. It will help you discover for yourself what Abraham discovered about grace, faith and obedience. Worksheets throughout the book make it useful as a personal or group study guide.

A Gentle & Quiet Spirit - Revised Edition

By Virginia Lefler

A NEW PERSPECTIVE FOR TODAY'S CHRISTIAN WOMAN

...the unfading beauty of a gentle and quiet spirit, which is
of great worth in God's sight.
- 1 Peter 3:4

Many Christian women face a dilemma in embracing the biblical teaching about a gentle and quiet spirit. They want to please God but they perceive "gentle" and "quiet" as weak or passive qualities. The truth is that the original Greek text describes a strong and peaceful woman, and the word translated "great worth" means the very end or limit with reference to value. In other words, there is nothing more valuable to God. This book will give you a new perspective and some valuable lessons in how to become this strong woman with inner peace. Twenty-five worksheets throughout the book make it especially useful as a personal or group study guide.

BOOKS AND TEACHING AIDS ARE AVAILABLE AT:

SilverdayPress.com

NOTES